DO YOU (YE)
NOW BELIEVE?

DO YOU (YE) NOW BELIEVE? NOW BELIEVE?

Believing GOD

W.N. Johnson

To order additional copies of this book, contact:
Xlibris Corporation
1-888-795-4274
www.Xlibris.com
Orders@Xlibris.com
38550

CONTENTS

Dedication

I prayerfully dedicate this book to my wife Barbara who continually encouraged and prayed with me as I tried to put my inspirations into print. I also want to include in my dedications my families, both immediate; consisting of my siblings and my children, my extended family known as the Cummings Family, and my spiritual family The Church of God.

ACKNOWLEDGEMENTS

I wish to thank a number of friends and relatives who encouraged me to continue with this writing. To my sisters, Everteen Ford, and Oreba Johnson who considers me their big brother I owe a great deal for their recognition of me as a preacher and minister of the word of God. I also wish to thank Pastor Dr. Derrick M. Thompson and the congregation of the First Church of God Harvey, for their support and fellowship for the past 6 or more years. My most humble thank you goes to our Heavenly Father and his son Jesus Christ for the Spiritual insight, strength, and revelation they have given me. To God be the glory, honor and increase for everything.

FOREWORD

DO YOU (YE) NOW BELIEVE?
St John 16:30,31

Having been involved in reading and studying the bible for well over 60 years, and having heard many interpretations of different parts of it, I have come to firmly believe that ***the bible means just what it says***. I believe that the bible is the inspired written word of the great creator God who brought all things into existence and keeps them in place by his power and might. I also believe that he is without equal; there is no power that can stand in competition to him. This being so, I am forced to believe that he is able to cause this word the bible to come down to us through many generations and yet say what he wants it to say to us, without our interpretations. I believe this so strongly that I am willing to stake my chance of receiving everlasting life upon it. I also believe that we are destined to ***inherit the*** *earth*, since this was the original purpose for which the creator made man. (Genesis 1; 26-28. To this very day I have not found a single scripture that ***promises heaven as a reward for the redeemed of the Lord;*** but the bible is literally full of scriptures promising the earth to the redeemed, even to the point of promising that ***God*** *himself will dwell with men in the New* ***Earth.*** Jesus promised that the comforter which is the ***Spirit of Truth*** would guide us into all truth. This same ***Spirit of Truth*** has guided me as I wrote these words contained in this book. I therefore wish to dedicate this book to the members of my immediate family, and also to my *Spiritual Family, The Church of God.*

BELIEVE AND RECEIVE EVERLASTING LIFE

"All things are possible to him that believeth" (Mark 9:23). 1 sincerely believe that God is frowning upon all those today who will not take him at his word. It is time for us to believe God, believe his word passed down to us through many generations. One case in point if you will: in Revelation chapter 5, verses 9 and 10 it is stated; **"And they sung a new song, saying,**

Thou art worthy to take the book, and to open the seals thereof: for thou wast slain, and hast redeemed us unto God by thy blood out of every kindred, and tongue, and people, and nation; and hast made us unto our God kings and priests: and we shall reign on the earth." Revelation 11:15 states; **"And the seventh Angel sounded, and there were great voices in heaven, saying, the kingdoms of this world are become the kingdoms of our Lord and of his Christ; and he shall reign forever and ever."** When I **read these scriptures and** many others including **Revelation *21:1-5*, I** can only **come** to one conclusion; that is that God is going to *restore the earth, set his **son** Jesus Christ over it as King of kings, and Lord of lords, and dwell **with men forever in the New Heaven and** Earth*. I know this is very difficult for the religions of this present world to conceive such an idea, especially since they have been deceived into believing that God desires to have them come up to heaven and dwell with him instead of what the written word is saying: *that God is going to come **down and dwell with men.***

I also want to remind the reader of the Holy Scripture to be aware of the warning recorded in Revelation the 22 and final chapter of the book, the bible, verses 18,19; **"For I testify unto every man that heareth the words of the prophecy of this book, if any man shall add unto these things, God shall add unto him the plagues that are written in this book: and if any man shall take away from the words of the book of this prophecy, God shall take away his part out of the book of life, and out of the Holy City, and from the things which are written in this book"** In view of these warnings I dare not read the scripture which says that *we have been redeemed to reign on the earth, and interpret it to mean we are going to Heaven.* (Revelation 5: 9, 10). So read on my friend at your own risk, and may the great creator God bless you to understand.

W.N.JOHNSON
Harvey, IL 60426

CHAPTER 1

God's Love Revealed
St. John 3:16

One of the main principals of salvation is belief. Let us take a good look at some of the scriptures where the word believe, believing, believeth, or believed appear in the Bible, called to be the word of God. One of the best known portions of scripture is found in St. John 3:12-18, especially verse 16 of this chapter which I now quote, **"For God so loved the world that he gave his only begotten son that whosoever believeth in him should not perish but have everlasting life."** Notice some key phrases, **"For God so loved the world."** Did you get it? I repeat, God so loved the world, not mankind, not the Heaven, not the fish, not the Sun, Moon, and Stars, not the Oceans and the Seas with their teaming life, not the Earth alone, but all of these together that make up our world. God loved it so much that he gave his only begotten Son that whosoever believeth in him should not perish.

Did you get the phrase **"should not perish?"** There must be something special about that word perish, especially since God would give his only begotten Son in order to give his creation a chance to avoid it. Webster's dictionary defines the word perish thus; ***to ruin or spoil; to suffer an untimely or violent death.*** The latter definition fits in exactly with what the creator warned Adam of in Genesis 2:16, 17. Notice the phrase thou shalt surely die. Note how this fits Webster's definition of perish**, *(suffer an untimely or violent death).*** God knew that Adam was formed of the dust of the ground and that he (God) had only breathed into his nostrils the breath (wind) of life and he (man) was just another of God's air breathing creatures who's existence depended upon the intake of air, food and water. God had not yet imparted unto the man *eternal or everlasting life.* To this very day man has not obtained *everlasting life,* although when God put the man into the garden *the tree of life* was there in the midst of the garden, along with the tree of the knowledge of good and evil. The man could have eaten of the tree of life had he chose to. God did not forbid his eating of the tree of life at this time. (Genesis 2:8, 9).

God commanded the man saying, **"Of every tree of the garden thou mayest freely eat. But of the tree of the knowledge of good and evil, thou shalt not eat of it: for in the day that thou eatest thereof thou shalt surely die."** (Genesis 2:16, 17). Adam had been given a choice, stay away from the tree of the knowledge of good and evil; obey God and live: or eat of the tree of the knowledge of good and evil; disobey God and die, (perish). But the serpent deceived Eve by telling her, you shall not surely die; just the opposite of what God the creator had said. It seems that she believed the serpent instead of God. The serpent lied to Eve, he told her, you shall not surely die, or in effect; you are an immortal soul, you can't really die, you will just become as wise as God. *Millions today still believe this lie.* If you believe that old statement, you must spend eternity somewhere, you are deceived. Let the word of God inform you on this matter; **"He that believeth on the Son hath everlasting life; and he that believeth not the Son shall not see life,** (everlasting life) **but the wrath of God abideth on him."** (John 3:36).

First we must realize that our present life is *temporal,* or subject to time. It is not *eternal or everlasting, nor immortal* as some would have you believe, so you shall not or will not spend eternity anywhere unless you believe on the Son of God. If you believe in him you have eternal life, if you do not believe in him you shall not have eternal life. Let God's word inform you of the state of the dead: **"For the living know that they shall die: but the dead know not anything, neither have they any more a reward, for the memory of them is forgotten. Also their love, and their hatred, and their envy, is now perished: neither have they any more a portion forever in anything that is done under the Sun."** (Ecclesiastes 9:5, 6). Did you get it? The dead know not anything, they don't have anything, and even their memory is forgotten. No burning forever in the so-called fires of hell, they just cease to exist.

The serpent did not communicate to Eve that God had not imparted to them his ever living Spirit but just the breath of life (wind). This is the same breath of life possessed by all of God's air breathing, fleshly creatures. Notice Ecclesiastes 3:17-20; **"I said in mine heart, God shall judge the righteous and the wicked; for there is a time there for every purpose, and for every work. I said in my heart concerning the estate of the sons of men, that God might manifest them, and that they might see that they themselves are beasts. For that which befalleth the sons of men befalleth beasts; even one thing befalleth them: as the one dieth, so dieth the other; Yea, they have all one breath; for all is vanity. All go unto one place; all are of the dust, and all turn to dust again."** Note also Genesis 3:19, 5:5; Hebrews 9:27; Psalms 146:3, 4; James 5:20. The word then does not proclaim that souls are immortal but rather that souls are perishable or subject to death. God knew the state of man from the beginning. In our present day world many have difficulty believing that there is an all powerful, all knowing, ever living creator; who is responsible for everything that exists.

GOD IS

David, in psalms 14:1, 53:1, says, **"The fool has said in his heart, there is no God."** How about you my friend? Have you said in your heart there is no God? You may deny that God does exist, but your denial does not make him go away or leave you alone. Listen to this word: **"For we shall all stand before the judgment seat of Christ, for it is written, as I live saith the Lord every knee shall bow to me, and every tongue shall confess to God."** (Romans 14:10b, 11). The choice is up to each individual. We can believe and inherit eternal life, or we can deny him (the Son of God) and perish. Notice; **"If we believe not, yet he abideth faithful: he cannot deny himself."** (2nd Timothy 2:13). This all wise, all powerful, ever present, all seeing, ever living creator has decreed that every knee shall bow and every tongue confess whether or not you believe him, or believe that he exists or not. Yes you may agree with those whom the word calls a fool, that God does not exist, but he says you will come face to face with him and you will acknowledge (confess) that he is Lord.

When I read in the bible about the orderly creation of things, and how the creator set them in place and assigned each a place in the universe as we know it; I stand in awe. I just begin to rejoice with the psalmist David: **"O Lord, our Lord, how excellent is thy name in all the earth! Who hast set thy glory above the heavens. Out of the mouth of babes and suckling hast thou ordained strength because of thine enemies, that thou mightiest still the enemy and the avenger. When I consider thy heavens, the work of thy fingers, the moon and the stars, which thou hast ordained; what is man, that thou art mindful of him? And the son of man that thou visitest him? For thou hast made him a little lower than the angels, and hast crowned him with glory and honor. Thou madest him to have dominion over the works of thine hands; thou hast put all things under his feet; all sheep and oxen, yea and the beasts of the field; The fowl of the air, and the fish of the seas. O Lord, our Lord, how excellent is thy name in all the earth!"** (Psalms 8).

My soul rejoices as I read about how he caused all things that we see, feel, smell, hear, and taste, to come into existence by saying, *"Let there be."*

Calling those things that did not exist into existence by speaking the word: *"Let there be light, let there be a firmament, let there be, etc. etc.* (Genesis chapter 1). **"The fool hath said in his heart, there is no God."** (Psalms 14:1). Yes my friend, only a fool can look around and see all the might and splendor of the universe surrounding him and say, there is no God. Nobody created or made all this it just happened. That is like finding a shiny Swiss watch on the ground, running and with the exact time of day and saying, there is no such thing as a Watchmaker, it just happened. But I believe in the Lord my God, creator and maker of all things. I agree with the prophets and writers of the Most High, who recorded this word and passed it down to us. **"Believe in the Lord your God, so shall ye be established; believe his prophets, so shall ye prosper."** (2 Chronicles 20:20b). My friend God is, whether you believe or not, notice the apostle's word in Romans 3:3; **"For what if some did not believe? Shall their unbelief make the faith of God without effect?** No my friend God is, always has been, always will be God.

THE PROPHETS ARE GOD'S SPOKESMEN

Everything that the Lord God does he reveals it to the prophets first. Concerning the redemption of his people, the Lord caused the prophet Isaiah to speak the following; **"Behold the Lord God will come with strong hand, and his arm shall rule for him: Behold his reward is with him and his work before him. He shall feed his flock like a shepherd: he shall gather the Lambs with his arms, and carry them in his bosom, and shall gently lead those that are with young. Who has measured the waters in the hollow of his hand, meted out heaven with the span, and comprehended the dust of the earth in a measure, and weighed the mountains in scales and the hills in a balance? Who hath directed the Spirit of the Lord, or being his counselor hath taught him? With whom took he counsel, and who instructed him, and taught in the path of judgment, and taught him knowledge, and shewed to him the way of understanding? Behold the nations are as a drop of a bucket, and are counted as the small dust of the balance: behold, he taketh up the isles as a very little thing. And Lebanon is not sufficient to burn, nor the beasts thereof sufficient for a burnt offering. All nations before him are as nothing and they are counted to him less than nothing and vanity. To whom then will ye liken God? Or what likeness will ye compare unto him? Have ye not known? Have ye not heard? Hath it not been told you from the beginning? Have ye not understood from the foundations of the earth? It is he that sitteth upon** the circle of the earth and the inhabitants thereof are as grasshoppers; That stretcheth out the heavens as a curtain and spreadeth them out as a tent to dwell in, that bringeth the princes to nothing; he maketh the judges of the earth as vanity. Yea they shall not be planted; they shall not be sown: yea, their stock shall not take root in the earth: and he shall also blow upon them, and they shall wither, and the whirlwind shall take them away as stubble. To whom then will ye liken me, or shall I be equal? Saith the Holy One. Lift up your eyes on high, and behold who hath created these things, that bringeth out their host by number: he calleth them all by names by the greatness of his might, for that he is strong in power; not one faileth. Why sayeth thou, O Jacob, and speakest, O Israel, My way is hid from the Lord, and my judgment is passed over from my God? Hast thou not known? Hast thou not heard that the everlasting God, the Lord, the creator of the ends of the earth, fainteth not neither is weary? There is no searching of his understanding." (Isaiah 40:10-28).

The creator continues to boast through the prophet Isaiah, **"I am the Lord and there is none else, there is no God beside me, I girded thee though thou hast not known me; that they may know from the rising of the sun and from the west, that there is none beside me, I am the Lord and there is none else. I form the light and create darkness: I make peace and create evil; I the Lord do all these things."** (Isaiah 45:5-7). Continuing: **"I have made the earth and created man upon it: I, even my hands have stretched out the heavens and all their host have I commanded. But Israel shall be saved in the Lord with an everlasting salvation; ye shall not be ashamed nor confounded world without end. For thus saith the Lord that created the heavens; God himself that formed the earth and made it, he hath established it, he created it not in vain, he formed it to be inhabited; I am the Lord and there is none else. I have not spoken in secret, in a dark place of the earth; I said not unto the seed of Jacob, seek ye me in vain: I the Lord speak righteousness; I declare things that are right. Look unto me, and be ye saved all the ends of the earth, for I am God and there is none else. I have sworn by myself, the word is gone out of my mouth in righteousness and shall not return, that unto me every knee shall bow every tongue shall swear."** (Isaiah 45:12, 17-19, 22, 23)

I believe the bible. I believe that it is the word of the all wise, all-powerful, ever living creator. I believe that he is wise and powerful enough to have this word come down to us and say what he wants it to say to us. St. John 3:15-17 tells us plainly that we do not have everlasting life, and if you want to obtain it for yourself all you have to do is believe in the son, on the son. Believe in his finished work, and believe that the Father God sent him to do this work, raised him up from the dead, and will send him back to earth again to restore all things, and reign forever as King of kings, and Lord of lords. The believer shall also reign with him. See St. John 14:1-12, Matthew 25:31-46, Revelation 5:9-10, 11:15, and Galatians 3:2.

CHAPTER 2

Believing God
Hebrews 10:35-39; 11:6

In the beginning of this discourse on believing we pointed out that the heart of God's plan for the salvation of mankind and the world centers around one principle in particular, *"believing on or in His only begotten son."* This fact is made clear in St. John 1:11-12, **"He came unto his own and his own received him not. But as many as received him to them he gave power to become the sons of God, even to them that believe in his name."** Again we quote from 1st John 5:10-12, **"He that believeth on the Son of God hath the witness in himself; he that believeth not God hath made him a liar, because he believeth not the record that God gave of his son. And this is the record that God hath given to us eternal life, and this life is in his Son. He that hath the Son hath life; and he that hath not the son of God hath not life."** Notice in these scriptures the following; **"to them gave he power to become the Sons of God," "this life is in his Son." "He that hath the Son hath life,"** and, **"he that hath not the Son hath not life."** I don't know how you could make this fact any clearer than it is in these statements. Either you believe and live, or don't believe and die. Since these words are written to people who are presently alive, it is clear to the sound mind that the life we now have is not permanent, that is to say, it won't last, and it is perishable. You would have to be a complete idiot not to recognize this fact, especially in view of the fact that we see people, our friends, loved ones, strangers, yes even animals and other creatures dying daily.

WHAT IT MEANS TO DIE

We need to understand what the meaning of death is**; to be dead is to cease to live.** Death is just the opposite of life, not life on some other planet; without life. We must not let false teachers, false prophets, or that old serpent the devil, the enemy of mankind, who comes to steal, kill, and destroy; fool us into thinking that we are, or that we have an immortal soul. If we, **"have not the Son"** (don't believe in him) we shall die. (Perish, cease to live). Let the Lord God himself tell you what death means; I repeat again **Ecclesiastes 9:5, "For the living know that they shall die but the dead know not anything; neither have they any more a reward; for the memory of them is forgotten."** Psalms 6:5; **"For in death there is no remembrance of thee; in the grave who shall give thee thanks."** Psalms 115:17; **"The dead praise not the Lord, neither any that go down into silence."** These are just a few of the definitions, or descriptions of the dead according to the bible. Webster's dictionary says to die means, *to cease to live,* to be dead is to be without life. *Death= extinction of life.* God knows these definitions to be true that is why he sent his only begotten Son so that we might have a choice through him. Make no mistake about it there is a work for you to do if you want to inherit everlasting life, that work is plainly stated in St. John 6:29: **"Jesus answered and said unto them, this is the work of God that ye** (you) **believe on him whom he hath sent."**

It is not surprising that so many do not believe that Jesus was and is the Son of God, especially when the word of God tells us in Hebrews 11:6, **"But without faith it is impossible to please him** (God) **for he that cometh to God must believe that he is and that he is a rewarder of them that diligently seek him."**

Many doubt that there is an all wise all knowing all powerful, ever present creator, who ever lives and sustains his creation. Certainly if you are not truly convinced that the creator God himself exists you cannot be convinced that he has a son who has the power to impart everlasting life. Be warned my friend; believe it or not the *creator lives;* and his son though crucified by evil men *lives also,* and sits on the right hand of the creator *interceding for the believer.* He waits the time appointed when the father shall send him forth to the earth again to restore all things. Acts 3:19-21; **"Repent ye therefore and be converted, that your sins may be blotted out, when the times of refreshing shall come from the presence of the Lord; and he shall send Jesus Christ, which before was preached unto you: whom the heaven must receive until the times of restitution of all things, which God hath spoken by the mouth of all his holy prophets since the world began."** Again I repeat; **do you now believe?** I urge you to believe God, believe on his son and live, more about this later.

BELIEVING GOD ABOUT LIFE AND DEATH
Ezekiel 18:4, 20; 37:12-14; Deut. 30:19.

"I have no pleasure in the death of him that dieth saith the Lord: wherefore turn yourselves and live ye." (Ezekiel 18:32). The creator tells us plainly that he is not pleased that any should perish (die). He proved this statement by sending forth his son to shed his righteous blood as the atonement for your sin and mine. **"All have sinned and come short of the glory of God."** (Romans 3:23). **"The wages of sin is death: but the gift of God is eternal life through Jesus Christ our Lord."** (Romans 6:23). Yes all have sinned, and what are we paid for our sin? Death, plain and simple. Not life in hell, or Hades, or any other place, but death, *without life.* Not just separation of body and spirit but the end of existence as a living soul. Contrary to the teaching of some false teachers, man does not have a soul he is a living soul. Genesis 2:7, **"And the Lord God formed man of the dust of the ground, and breathed into his nostrils the breath of life and man *BECAME* a living soul."** Notice; he was not given a soul, he *BECAME* a living soul. The dust and the breath together became a living soul, just as the other beings that God had created and given the breath of life. Souls die; *"The soul that sinneth, it shall die."* (Ezekiel 18:4). So that you would not think that this was a mistake or a misprint it is repeated again in verse 20; and in Romans 6:23a. Do you believe that souls die? God says that they die, *that is ceased to live,* and I believe God.

See Genesis 6:7; **"And the Lord said, I will destroy man whom I have created from the face of the earth."** To destroy means to put an end to, or turn to rubble. Notice Genesis 6:13, **"And God said unto Noah, the end of all flesh is come up before me; for the earth is filled with violence through them. And behold I will destroy them with the earth."** Notice in particular the word *destroy*, which means, put an end to. So according to the great creator God, man and the earth from which he was taken can be destroyed. If they can be destroyed then they are not immortal. Immortal means *undying, deathless, "one exempt from death or decay."*

No my friend, you are not an immortal soul as the enemy Satan would have you believe. He deceived Eve by telling her that if she disobeyed God she would not really die. (Genesis 3:4, 5). God had said to Adam, **"In the day that thou eateth thereof, thou shalt surely die."** (Genesis 2:17). Adam and Eve should have believed God instead of listening to that old serpent the devil. Let us look at some more scriptures that tell us about ourselves; **"Behold,** all souls are mine, as the soul of the father, so also the soul of the son is mine; the soul that sinneth it shall die." First the creator boasted, *"All souls are mine,"* surely you can understand that for he created them. The word create means to bring into existence out of nothing. So he has the right by virtue of his bringing them into existence to boast, *"All souls are mine,"* but he also warns, **"The soul that sinneth, it shall die."** So important is it that you understand that principle, God had it repeated again and again. **"Sin is the transgression of the law."** (1 John 3:4b). Transgress means to violate the law, so when we violate the law we sin. The penalty for sin is *death.*

GOD DOES NOT WANT US TO DIE

The loving, merciful, longsuffering, creator of the universe is concerned about his creation. So concerned that he has put in motion a plan whereby he might preserve his creation. Notice the Lord's concern in the following scriptures, **"I call heaven and earth to record this day against you that I have set before you, life and death, blessing and cursing; therefore choose life that thou and thy seed may live."** (Deuteronomy 30:19). Here he advises, choose life. Listen again; **"If the wicked will turn from all his sins that he hath committed, and keep all my statures, and do that which is lawful and right, he shall surely live, he shall not die. All his transgressions that he hath committed, they shall not be mentioned unto him: in his righteousness that he hath done he shall live."** (Ezekiel 18:21, 22). God wants to forgive, he wants to forget, yes, forgive and forget. Why? Listen to him explain; **"Have I any pleasure at all that the wicked should die? Saith the Lord God, and not that he should return from his ways and live? But when the righteous turneth away from his righteousness, and committeth iniquity and doeth according to all the abominations that the wicked man doeth, shall he live? All his righteousness that he hath done shall not be mentioned: in his trespass that he hath trespassed, and in his sin that he hath sinned, in them shall he die. Yet ye say, the way of the Lord is not equal. Hear now, O house of Israel; is not my way equal? Are not your ways unequal? When a righteous man turneth away from his righteousness and commmitteth iniquity and dieth in them; for his iniquity that he hath done shall he die. Again, when the wicked man turneth away from his wickedness that he hath committed and doeth that which is lawful and right, he shall save his soul alive. Because he considereth and turneth away from all his transgressions that he hath committed, he shall surely live, he shall not die."** (Ezekiel 18:20-28).

The merciful creator God, does not want his work to perish, (die). The Apostle Peter wrote; **"The lord is not slack concerning his promise, as some men count slackness; but is longsuffering to usward, not willing that any should perish, but that all should come to repentance."** (2 Peter 3:9). To repent means to turn around, or change direction, notice the words, **"considereth and turneth away from."** (Ezekiel 18:28). That is repentance in action. The creator says that if a man does this; repents, turn away from sin, and transgression of the law, "he shall surely live, he shall not die." Notice Peter's words, **especially *long suffering*;** God will go to great lengths to preserve his creation, not just mankind, but also the whole world. (John 3:16). Also remember that nothing is too hard for God. (Jeremiah 32:17, 27). **"With God all things are possible."** (Mark 10:27b). And for him that believeth, **"all things are possible."** (Mark 9:23, 24). **"Lord I believe, help thou mine unbelief."** (Verse 24).

EXERCISING DOMINION OVER DEATH

When Jesus was told that Lazarus, his friend whom he loved, was sick, (the brother of Mary and Martha) he deliberately stayed where he was for another two days and then said to his disciples, **"Our friend Lazarus sleepeth but I go that I may awake him out of sleep. His disciples said, Lord if he sleeps he shall do well."** They thought Jesus meant that he was resting as is common with men, but Jesus said to them, **"Lazarus is dead."** Notice his next remarks, **"And I am glad for your sakes that I was not there, to the intent ye may believe; never the less let us go unto him."** (John 11:11-15). With just a little imagination you can just see the bewildered look on the face of his disciples as they thought; it won't do any good to go to him now, and he's dead already. Jesus could have rushed to the aid of his friends, but he did not, instead he deliberately waited until Lazarus had died and then went unto them. The events that followed were absolutely astounding. Jesus found that Lazarus had been dead four days and was already buried. His actions brought out the fact that even these close friends had not yet accepted the truth about who he really was. **"Then Martha, as soon as she heard that Jesus was coming, went and met him but Mary sat still in the house. Then said Martha unto Jesus, Lord if thou hadst been here, my brother had not died. But I know, that even now, whatsoever thou wilt ask of God, God will give it thee. Jesus saith unto her, thy brother shall rise again. Martha saith unto, him I know that he shall rise again in the resurrection at the last day. Jesus saith unto her, I am the resurrection** and the life, he that believeth on me, though he were dead, yet shall he live; and whosoever liveth and believeth in me shall never die. Believeth thou this? She saith unto him, yea Lord, I believe that thou art the Christ, the son of God, which should come into the world, And when she had so said she went her way and called Mary her sister secretly, saying, The master is come and calleth for thee. As soon as she heard that, she arose quickly and came unto him." Mary came with the same remarks as her sister Martha; "Lord, if thou had been here my brother had not died." (Vs 32b). "Jesus groaned in the spirit and was troubled; (notice the small (s) in spirit) And said, Where have ye laid him? They said unto him, Lord, come and see. Jesus wept." When he arrived at the grave he again groaned in himself. "Jesus said, Take ye away the stone." Again unbelief sprang up in Martha, for she sought to intervene by saying, "Lord by this time he stinketh; for he hath been dead four days. Jesus saith unto her, said I not unto thee, that, If thou wouldest believe, thou shouldest see the glory of God. Then they took away the stone from the place where the dead was laid, and Jesus lifted up his eyes, and said, Father, I thank thee that thou hast heard me. And I knew that thou hearest me always: but because of the people which stand by I said it, that they may believe that thou hast sent me. And when he thus had spoken, he cried with a loud voice, LAZARUS COME FORTH. And he that was dead came forth, bound hand and foot with grave clothes, and his face was bound about with a napkin. Jesus saith unto them, loose him and let him go." (St. John 11:32-44).

Lazarus came forth even though he was still bound hand and foot, demonstrating that Jesus through his Father had power over death. Mary and Martha's tears of sorrow suddenly turned into tears of joy, as they removed the grave clothes from their brother and examined him, and found that he was completely whole. Perhaps they could now understand **Jesus repeatedly stating to them, "He that believeth in me, though he were dead, yet shall he live."** (St. John 11:25).

"ANOTHER WITNESS"

We have other witnesses to the fact of God's resurrection powers, let us bring to the witness stand one of the prophets of old; Ezekiel. The creator carried Ezekiel out and sat him down in the midst of the valley of dry bones, and asked him; "Son of man, can these bones live?" Ezekiel answered, "O Lord God, thou knowest." Again he said unto me, Prophesy upon these bones and say unto them, O ye dry bones, hear the word of the

Lord. Thus saith the Lord God unto these bones; Behold I will cause breath to enter into you, and ye shall live; And I will lay sinews upon you, and will bring up flesh upon you, and cover you with skin, and put breath in you, and ye shall live: and ye shall know that I am the Lord. So I prophesied as I was commanded: and as I prophesied, there was a noise, and behold a shaking, and the bones came together, bone to his bone. And when I beheld, lo the sinews and the flesh came up upon them and the skin covered them above; but there was no breath in them. Then said he unto me, Prophesy unto the wind, prophesy, Son of man, and say to the wind, Thus saith the Lord God; come from the four winds O breath, and breathe upon these slain that they may live. So I prophesied as he commanded me, and the breath came into them and they lived, and stood up upon their feet, an exceeding great army.** (Ezekiel 37:1-10). The creator God demonstrated to the prophet his power in the Spirit. The dry bones the Lord informed Ezekiel, **are the whole house of Israel, behold, they say, our bones are dried, and our hope is lost: we are cut off for our parts. Therefore prophesy and say unto them, thus saith the Lord God; behold, O my people, I will open your graves, and cause you to come up out of your graves, and bring you into the land of Israel. And ye shall know that I am the Lord, when I have opened your graves, O my people, and brought you up out of your graves. And shall put my spirit in you, and ye shall live, and I shall place you in your own land: then shall ye know that, I the Lord have spoken it, and performed it, saith the Lord.** (Ezekiel 37:11-14). Compare this with Revelation 20:4, 12, 13, and also with St. John 5:24-29.

BELIEVING GOD ABOUT THE RESURRECTION

The scribes and Pharisees were among the most critical of Jesus during his tenure here on earth. They were constantly seeking to trap him either in word or deed. So it was nothing new to him when they confronted him saying; **"Master we would see a sign from thee, But he answered and said unto them, an evil and adulterous generation seeketh after a sign; and there shall no sign be given to it, but the sign of the prophet Jonas: For as Jonas was three days and three nights in the whales belly; so shall the Son of Man be three days and three nights in the heart of the earth."** (Matthew 12:38-40). Notice the phrase, **three days and three nights.** Jesus pointed out to them that they could prove he was the messiah by comparing his stay in the grave with Jonas stay in the belly of the whale. In the eleventh chapter of St. John Jesus stated, and I quote; **"Are there not twelve hours in a day?"** Since there are twenty-four hours in a whole day as described in Genesis, three days and three nights are equal to seventy-two hours, *three twelve hour nights (evening) and three twelve hour days (morning).* Jesus did remain in the heart of the earth seventy-two hours, if he did not, then according to his own words he was not the messiah. Do you believe him? If you believe him, then you know that the Friday evening burial and the Sunday morning resurrection is a hoax. A lie put forth by the enemy and practiced by millions of people today. The same enemy that said to Eve; **"You shall not surely die."** It is time now for us to take God at his word. He knows what he wants to say, and means what he says. Hear his word through the prophet; **"I the Lord speak righteousness, I declare things that are right."** (Isaiah 45:19b). His word will stand, **"Heaven and earth shall pass away, but my words shall not pass away."** (Matthew 24:35). **"Sanctify them through thy truth, thy word is truth."** (St. John 17:17). In spite of this sign, which Jesus gave them, they did not believe that he was the Son of God, the Holy one of Israel, the promised Messiah.

THEY DID NOT BELIEVE HIM!

Even after his words came to pass, unbelief clouded the mind of many of his closest friends. Notice St. Luke 24, beginning at the very first verse; **"Now upon the first day of the week very early in the morning, they came to the sepulcher, bringing the spices which they had prepared, and certain others with them. And they found the stone rolled away from the sepulcher. And they entered in, and found not the body of the Lord Jesus. And it came to pass, that as they were much perplexed there about, behold, two men stood by them in shining garments: And as they were afraid, and bowed down their faces to the earth, they said unto them, why seek ye the living among the dead? He is not here, but is risen: remember how he spake unto you when he was yet in Galilee, saying, the son of man must be delivered into the hands of sinful men, and be crucified, and the third day rise again. And they remembered his words, and returned from the sepulcher, and told all these things unto the eleven and to all the rest. It was Mary Magdalene, and Joanna, and Mary the mother of James, and other women that were with them, which told these things unto the apostles. And their words seemed to them as idle tales, and they believed them not."** (St. Luke 24:1-11). If the women had believed Jesus' words they would not have gone to the trouble of preparing spices and traveling all the way to the grave site; they would have known that he would not be there, since three days and three nights had already passed. The men who stood by them in shining garments were evidently angels, sent by God himself to testify of the resurrection of his Son, so now having received the testimony of the heavenly witnesses the women hastened to tell the apostles.

WHAT ABOUT THE APOSTLES?

The following scriptures demonstrate the extent of the apostle's disbelief. "Then arose Peter and ran unto the sepulcher, and stooping down, he beheld the linen clothes laid by themselves, and departed, wondering in himself at that which was come to pass. And behold, two of them went that same day to a village called Emmaus, which was from Jerusalem about threescore furlongs. And it came to pass that while they communed together and reasoned, Jesus himself drew near, and went with them. But their eyes were holden that they should not know him. And he said unto them, what manner of communications are these that ye have one to another, as ye walk, and are sad? And one of them whose name was Cleopas answering said unto him, Art thou only a stranger in Jerusalem, and hast not known the things which are come to pass there in these days? And he said unto them, what things? And they said unto him, concerning Jesus of Nazareth, which was a prophet mighty in deed and word before God and all the people: And how the chief priests and our rulers delivered him to be condemned to death, and have crucified him. But we trusted that it had been he, which should have redeemed Israel: and beside all this, today is the third day since all these thing were done. Yea, and certain women also of our company made us astonished which were early at the sepulcher. And when they found not his body, they came saying, that they had also seen a vision of angels, which said that he was alive. And certain of them, which were with us, went to the sepulcher, and found it even as the women had said; but him they saw not. Then he said unto them, O fools and slow of heart to believe all that the prophets have spoken, ought not Christ to have suffered these things, and to enter into his glory? (St. Luke 24:12-26). Continuing at verse 30; And it came to pass, as he sat at meat with them, he took bread, and blessed it, and brake, and gave to them, and their eyes were opened, and they knew him; and he vanished out of their sight. And they said one to another, did not our heart burn within us, while he talked with us by the way, and while he opened to us the scriptures? (Verses 30-32). Notice; they walked

15

and talked with him on the road to Emmaus, yet they did not know him. So disappointed were they that Jesus had not restored Israel back to her pomp and splendor as she once was under David and Solomon that they could not even think on the words he had spoken unto them, let alone believe them. This indeed is one of mankind's greatest faults. We are so busy figuring out what God is going to do next, or what he meant by the things he said, that we miss the mark altogether. Had they: and in this case *they* would include, the Scribes, Pharisees, the eleven disciples in particular, Mary Magdalene, Joanna, Mary the mother of James, the chief priests, and rulers of the people; had they believed his words, then first of all the scribes and Pharisees would have known that he was the one of whom the prophets spoke.

The disciples would have expected him to rise again after three days, Peter would not have denied him three times, the women would not have made the pilgrimage to the sepulcher, for they would have been assured that he was no longer there. Can you hear the Masters voice today shouting to all his would be followers; **"O fools and slow to believe all that the prophets have spoken."** (St. Luke 24:25). Yes my friend, just as they would not believe Jesus, or his words back then, millions of those claiming to be Christians today do not believe him or his words today. Notice the condemnation spoken by Jesus**, "The men of Nineveh shall rise up in judgment with this generation, and shall condemn it; because they repented at the preaching of Jonas; and behold a greater than Jonas is here. The Queen of the south shall rise up in the judgment with this generation, and shall condemn it; for she came from the utmost parts of the earth to hear the wisdom of Solomon; and behold, a greater than Solomon is here."** Why such condemnation? Because they heard the words direct from the Master himself. Notice; **"A greater than Jonas is here." "A greater than Solomon is here."** Notice also his words, **"Three days and three nights."** Today millions follow the popular Easter doctrine which predicts a Friday evening crucifixion and a before daybreak Sunday morning resurrection. If you follow this doctrine, you make Jesus a liar, for he said that he would be *three days and three nights in the heart of the earth.* That's a total of seventy-two (72) hours. Does it matter? Some will say that it doesn't matter, but as for me, Jesus said it, I believe it, and that settles it so far as I am concerned. All the enemy has to offer will not convince me to think differently.

Remember Eve? If Jesus was wrong about being three days and three nights (72 hours) in the grave, then he could also be wrong about going to prepare a place for believers, and coming back to receive them unto himself. Notice; **"Let not your heart be troubled, ye believe in God, believe also** in me. **In my father's house are many mansions: if it were not so I would have told you. I go to prepare a place for you. And if I go and prepare a place for you I will come again, and receive you unto myself; that where I am there ye may be also."** (St. John 11:25, 26). Again I submit that, if Jesus was in error about the time of his burial in the heart of the earth, then he could be in error about the resurrection altogether.

CHAPTER 3

The Resurrection Is A Sure Thing
Jesus Made It Plain

Notice these plain statements from the Lord Jesus himself, **"Marvell not at this; for the hour is coming in the which all that are in the graves shall hear his voice, and shall come forth; they that have done good, unto the resurrection of life, and they that have done evil, unto the resurrection of damnation."** (St. John 5:28, 29). Also notice: **"Jesus said unto her I am the resurrection and the life: he that believeth in me, though he were dead, yet shall he live; and whosoever liveth and believeth in me shall never die. Believeth thou this?"** (St. John 11:25, 26). Yes my friend I truly believe that Jesus is the resurrection and the life. When he calls all will come forth, no matter how long they have been dead, no matter where are how they died. I believe those he calls to life will receive everlasting life at that time.

The prophets of old, Abraham, Isaac, Jacob, and the apostles of Jesus day all await the sound of the voice of the Son of man, for they are all dead at present. Notice the scriptural proof of this fact; **"These all died in faith, not having received the promises."** (Hebrews 11:13). Notice the Apostle Paul's writings on the subject of the resurrection; **"Now if Christ be preached that he rose from the dead, how say some among you that there is no resurrection of the dead? But if there be no resurrection of the dead, then is Christ not risen; and if Christ be not risen, then is our preaching vain, and your faith is also vain, yea, and we are found false witnesses of God; for we have testified of God that he raised up Christ: whom he raised not up if so be that the dead rise not. For if the dead rise not, then is Christ not raised; and if Christ be not raised, your faith is vain; ye are yet in your sin. Then they also which are fallen asleep in Christ are perished. If in this life only we have hope in Christ, we are of all men most miserable. But now is Christ risen from the dead, and become the first fruits of them that slept. For since by man came death, by man came also the resurrection of the dead. For as in Adam all die, even so in Christ shall all be made**

alive. But every man in his own order: Christ the first fruits; afterwards they that are Christ's at his coming." 1 Corinthians15:12-23).

Abraham has not ascended up to heaven. What a shock to some of those seeking to go to heaven. Your bible and mine, if you are using a King James Version, which is common today, plainly tells us that the patriarchs and prophets of old, though faithful, are now dead. Hebrews chapter eleven is a listing of many of the servants of the Most High God, men and women, who in spite of their faithfulness, died without receiving the fullness of the promises mad to them by the great creator God. I quote from Hebrews 11:13; **"These all died in faith, not having received the promises, but having seen them afar off, and were persuaded of them, and embraced them, and confessed that they were strangers and pilgrims on the earth."** Yes they died, that is they ceased to live, and are still dead to this very day. Make no mistake about it, these servants of the Most High God are dust today. I know this is very hard for those who have been taught to believe that they have an immortal soul, but God never said that man has an immortal soul, that idea came from another source, the serpent. (Genesis 3:4). God commanded the man saying, **"Of every tree of the garden thou mayest freely eat: but the tree of the knowledge of good and evil, thou shalt not eat of it; for in the day that thou eatest thereof thou shalt surely die."** (Genesis 2:16, 17). God informed Adam that he would *surely die*, not be moved off to some place where he could not be seen, or outside of God as some put it, *but die, that is cease to live.* God said that he (Adam) would return to the ground: **"In the sweat of thy face shalt thou eat bread, till thou return unto the ground; for out of it wast thou taken: for dust thou art,** (not immortal soul or spirit) **and unto dust shalt thou return."** (Genesis 3:19). So not only are these faithful ones dead, but they have not yet received the *fullness of the promises* made by the creator God. One of these promises is *everlasting life.* It is also obvious that they are not in heaven, because hundreds of years after they died, Jesus came on the scene and stated, **"And no man hath ascended up to heaven but he that came down from heaven even the Son of man which is in heaven."** (St. John 3 13).

WHERE ARE ABRAHAM AND THE PATRIARCHS?

Let the word answer this question for you. We have already determined from the words of Jesus that they are not in heaven. We have also determined from Hebrews 11 that they all died. What happens to one who dies? Let us see if we can find out by searching the scriptures what happened to

Abraham. From the book of Genesis we read the following: **"And these are the days of the years of Abraham's life which he lived, an hundred three score and fifteen years. Then Abraham gave up the ghost and died in a good old age, an old man and full of years, and was gathered to his people. And his sons Isaac and Ishmael buried him in the cave of Machpelah, in the field of Ephron the son of Zohar the Hittite, which is before Mamre; the field which Abraham purchased of the sons of Heth: there was Abraham buried, and Sarah his wife."** (Genesis 25:7-10). We now know where Abraham is according to God's word the bible. It is interesting to note that the bible record does not say that *Abraham's sons buried Abraham's body* in the cave of Machpelah, it says they buried *Abraham*; his wife *Sarah* was already buried there. They are still dead unto this very day, your bible says so.

Let us consider another Patriarch, David: who is called in the bible, **"A man after God's own heart."** (1 Samuel 13:14; Acts 13:22). If any man made it up to heaven, surely this man David would be the one, or at least among the ones to get there. And certainly there had been plenty of time for him to have traveled from the city of David up to heaven by the time that Peter preached his first sermon on the day of Pentecost. But notice Peter's testimony concerning David: **"Men and brethren, let me freely speak unto you of the patriarch David, that he is 'both dead and buried, and his sepulcher is with us unto this day."** (Acts 2:29). Yes, my friend, nearly one thousand years after the death of David, the Holy Ghost reveals through the apostle Peter that David is still *dead and buried*. Notice also that the Holy Ghost did not make any distinctions, he did not say that David's body was dead and buried, or any other part of him, he said David the man. But how could this be some will ask? Let the prophet Jeremiah tell you; **"But they shall serve the Lord their God, and David their king, whom I will raise up unto them."** (Jeremiah 30:9). These words were spoken through Jeremiah the prophet; by the one called Lord, who later became Jesus. Hear his word as Jesus: **"Verily, verily, I say unto you, the hour is coming and now is, when the dead shall hear the voice of the son of God, and they that hear shall live."** (John 5:25). Did you get the connection? Notice Jeremiah 30:9, **"David their king whom I will raise up unto them."** David had been dead for years when Jeremiah wrote this. Note also, **"The dead shall hear the voice of the son of God."** David will be one of those who will hear the voice of the son of God. But for the present, whether you believe it or not, *Abraham and David are dead.* Peter continues, **"For David is not ascended into the heavens."** (Plural, so this means all the heavens) (Acts 2:34b). Understand what you have read my friend; even though Abraham and David are now dead, when Jesus calls them they will live again. It does not matter how long they have been dead, nor, how or why they died. Even though their bodies have returned to dust, and the dust scattered all over the face of the Universe, when Jesus calls and the Trumpet sounds, the dust will get together and stand up before the Lord. See Daniel 12:2; 1 Corinthians 15:51, 52; 1 Thessalonians 4:13-18; Revelations 20:11-15.

THE RESURRECTION IS A SURE THING

Believe God, believe his prophets, and believe his Son. The resurrection of the dead is a sure thing according to your bible and mine. And since it is sure, the patriarchs all await the voice of the Son of God, at which time they will receive their immortal bodies, and assume their appointed place in the Kingdom of God. I know there are those who will try to persuade you to believe that all those who have preceded us in death, especially if they were converted believers, are now with the Lord, but the bible tells us different. I believe the bible is the written word of the great creator God; handed down to us through many generations, and *I choose to believe what it says,* the way it says it. In keeping with the bible's teachings about the resurrection of the dead we can see why the apostle Paul made the following statements in his letter to the Philippians; **"But what things were gain to me, those I counted loss for Christ. Yea doubtless, and I count all things but loss for the excellency of the knowledge of Christ Jesus my Lord: for whom I have suffered the loss of all things, and do count them but dung, that I may win Christ. And be found in him, not having mine own righteousness which is of the law, but that which is through the faith of Christ, the righteousness which is of God by faith: That I may know him, and the power of his resurrection, and the fellowship of his sufferings, being made conformable unto his death; If by any means I might attain unto the resurrection of the dead."** (Philippians 3:7-11).

Why is the attaining of the resurrection of the dead so important to the apostle Paul? The resurrection from the dead and the change are two things that separate Jesus from all the others who were raised from the dead. The others later died again. They had their physical bodies restored to life, the blood, which is the life of the mortal flesh, once again flowed through their bodies, they once again breathed air in and out of their lungs supplying oxygen to that blood; that is, all except Jesus. Jesus remains alive forever more. There was something very special about Jesus after his resurrection, note: **"Jesus saith unto her, touch me not; for I am not yet ascended to my father; but go to my brethren and say unto them, I ascend unto my father and your father, and to my God and your God."** (John 20:17). Notice the words **"touch me not."** It must have been important that he, be not touched by human hands before he ascended unto his father, but let us see what happened later. **"Then the same day at evening, being the first day of the week, when the doors were shut where the disciples were assembled for fear of the Jews, came Jesus and stood in the midst, and saith unto them, peace be unto you. And when he had so said, he shewed unto them his hands and his side."** (John 20:19, 20). Jesus body was the same as when they placed him in the sepulchere, the nail prints in his hand, the spear mark in his side. **"And after eight days again his disciples were within and Thomas with them.** (Thomas had not been with them when Jesus appeared the first time unto them). **Then came Jesus the door being shut and stood in the midst and said, peace be unto you. Then saith he to Thomas reach hither thy finger, and behold my hands; and reach hither thy hand, and thrust it into my side; and be not faithless but believing."** This was without a doubt the same Jesus who had been nailed to the cross and speared in the side by the Roman soldiers, for Thomas answered, **"My Lord and My God."** (John 20:28b).

Let us read St. Luke's account of this same incident; **"And as they thus spake, Jesus himself stood in the midst of them, and saith unto them, peace be unto you. But they were terrified and affrighted, and supposed that they had seen a spirit.**

And he said unto them, why are ye troubled? And why do thoughts arise in your hearts? Behold my hands and my feet, that it is I myself: handle me, and see; for a spirit hath not flesh and bones as ye see me have." (Luke 24:36-39). Did you notice any thing different as we read Luke's account of this incident? Let me point out something to you. Number one, in John's account Jesus said to Mary Magdalene, "Touch me not." This was early in the morning while it was yet dark; but later that same day he allowed them to handle him, even inviting Thomas to thrust his hand into his side, which is evidence that the hole left by the spear was still there. This act was enough to convince even doubting Thomas, and he answered and said **"my Lord and my God."** (John 20:28). Keep this in mind, same body, same nail prints, same spear marks, but according to Luke's account there was something missing, something different with this body. Notice the words of Jesus; **"A spirit hath not flesh and bones as ye see me have."** (Luke 24:39). Did you notice, he made no mention of blood? The very thing that is the life of the flesh is missing. (Genesis 7:4; Leviticus 17:14). Yet this is the same body; it has been changed, it does not contain blood, just flesh and bones.

Yes my friend, this body has now undergone the change that the apostle Paul wrote to the Corinthians about. **"Now this I say, brethren, that flesh and blood cannot inherit the Kingdom of God; neither doth corruption inherit incorruption, behold I shew you a mystery; we shall not all sleep but we shall all be changed. In a moment, in the twinkling of an eye, at the last trump; for the trumpet shall sound, and the dead shall be raised incorruptible, and we shall be changed."** (1 Corinthians 15:50-52).

It is quite evident that the body of Jesus had undergone this change. He could now pass through stone, and wood, even other human bodies with ease. That is how he suddenly appeared unto the disciples standing in the midst of them, even though the doors were shut. Jesus is the first to go through this process and be born into the kingdom of God. It is no mystery then, if you understand this process, to understand why the apostle Paul would be willing to, and did, count all that he had accomplished, as nothing in order to **"attain unto the resurrection of the dead."** By this process Jesus became, **"the firstborn of many brethren."** (Romans 8:29). Up until this time no man had been born into the kingdom of God, no not one, Jesus became the first. (John 3:13; 20:17). The resurrection from the dead, and the change are clearly the door leading to everlasting life, through which the man Jesus entered. (1 Corinthians 15:51, 52). Hear and believe his testimony; **"Then said Jesus unto them again; verily, verily, I say unto you, I am the door of the sheep. All that ever came before me are thieves, and robbers: But the sheep did not hear them; I am the door: by me if any man enter in he shall be saved, and shall go in and out and find pasture."** (John 10:7-9). **"Jesus saith unto him, I am the way, the truth, and the life: no man cometh to the father, but by me." (John 14:6).** That is why the apostle Paul was willing to sacrifice every thing, just so that he might, **"know him,** (Jesus), **and the power of his resurrection, and the fellowship of his sufferings, being made conformable unto his death. If by any means I might attain unto the resurrection of the dead."** (Philippians 3:10, 11). Believe God my friend, believe his word, believe his prophets, and inherit everlasting life.

CHAPTER 4

Jesus Is Coming Again

WHAT IS MAN?

As I continue with this series on believing and receiving, I feel a compelling urge to point out at this time some of the things revealed unto me about the state of man. In Psalms chapter eight the Psalmist points out an important fact that we need to know about the state of man. Listen: **"What is man, that thou art mindful of him? And the son of man that thou visiteth him? For thou hast made him a little lower than the angels, and hast crowned him with glory and honor."** (Psalms 8:4, 5). Notice, **"a little lower than the angels."** And how has he made the angels? We find one answer in the book of Hebrews chapter one, **"But to which of the angels said he at any time, sit on my right hand, until I make thine enemies thy footstool? Are they not all ministering spirits, sent forth to minister for them who shall be heirs of salvation?"** (Hebrews 1:13, 14*). Angels were made, ministering spirits, man was not.* He was made a little lower, and being made lower, he is subject to death *(cease to live, not get out of the body and continue to live as a spirit, but cease to live).* Until you can believe that *men really die*, you will not believe that *Jesus died*, and was dead for three days and three nights. And if you cannot *believe that he was dead*, then there is no grounds for a resurrection in your case scenario, and that my friend automatically excludes you from entering into the Kingdom of God's dear Son and receiving everlasting life. **"If thou shalt confess with thy mouth the Lord Jesus, and shalt believe in thine heart that God hath raised him from the dead, thou shalt be saved."** (Romans 10:9). God knows what he is doing, his wisdom is past finding out by finite beings like you and I, but some things he reveals to those who will believe and accept, and seek his face. It is really amazing how many of God's plans and works he has revealed in his word the bible. Yet we fail to grasp them because we do not want to believe him. What a marvelous thing the Father God has put into place for men. He first creates him a little lower than the angels, knowing that man would sin and bring death upon himself and his descendants, he devised a way to redeem him. Had God not brought his plan into existence, Satan would have brought an end to mankind there in the Garden of Eden. But what better way to deal with this situation than to have a man live out his tenure, and then die (fall asleep), while preparation for his redemption is carried out. Then at the appointed time awake him, change him, and empower him for his original charge. Can you just imagine how many people would be on the earth today if Adam and Eve and all their descendants were still here? We would have wall to wall people, the earth would be overrun with flesh and blood creatures. More about this later, let it suffice for now that we need the resurrection and the change in order to enter into the *Kingdom of our Lord and his Christ. Not all will die (sleep), but all must be changed.*(1 Corinthians 15:20-26, 51).

THE SECOND COMING OF JESUS CHRIST
Matthew 6:9-13, Revelations 22:20

As I meditated on how to continue with the revelations given me on believing and receiving, it came up in my mind to start this section off with a phrase from the sixth chapter of Matthew, ***"Thy Kingdom come."*** It took me quite some time to recognize the connection involved with Believing and Receiving, but as is the case with many things involving Spiritual discernment I had to remain in meditation until it began to open up to me. You see, the final portion of Jesus mission has not yet been brought into being. He came, **"to minister and to give his life a ransom for many."** (Matthew 20:28b; Mark 10:45b). This he has already done on Calvary, but that is not all he was predestined to do. Let the apostle Peter tell us about it; **"Those things which God before had shewed by the mouth of all his prophets, that Christ should suffer, he hath so fulfilled. Repent ye therefore and be converted, that your sins may be blotted out, when the times of refreshing shall come from the presence of the Lord: And he shall send Jesus Christ, which before was preached unto you: whom the heaven must receive until the times of restitution of all things, which God hath spoken by the mouth of all his holy prophets since the world began."** (Acts 3:18-21).

Here in Peter's message is a key revelation, notice, **"Those things that Christ should suffer."** I can think of no better description of the things that Christ should suffer than that given by the prophet Isaiah. I quote; **"Who hath believed our report? And to whom is the arm of the Lord revealed? For he shall grow up before him as a tender plant, and as a root out of** dry ground: he hath no form nor comeliness; and when we shall see him, there is no beauty that we should desire him. He is despised and rejected of men; a man of sorrows and acquainted with grief: and we hid as it were our faces from him; he was despised, and we esteemed him not. Surely he hath borne our griefs, and carried our sorrows; Yet we did esteem him 'stricken, smitten of God and afflicted. But he was wounded for our transgressions, he was bruised for our iniquities; the chastisement of our peace was upon him; and with his stripes we are healed. All we like sheep have gone astray; we have turned every one to his own way; And the Lord hath laid on him the iniquity of us all. He was oppressed, he was afflicted, yet he opened not his mouth. He was taken from prison and from judgment; and who shall declare his generation? For he was cut off out of the land of the living; for the transgressions of my people was he stricken.** (Isaiah 53:1-8). We read this account of the sufferings prophesied of the Messiah and say, "oh my what a way to go." And just think, he went through all this torture for your sin and mine. Then we read in verse 9," **He had done no violence, neither was any deceit in his mouth. Yet it pleased the Lord to bruise him; he hath put him to grief: when thou shalt make his soul an offering for sin, he shall see his seed, he shall prolong his days, and the pleasure of the Lord shall prosper in his hand.**" (Isaiah 53:9b, 10). There can be no doubt as to whom these scriptures apply, but this portion of scripture has been satisfied as Peter proclaims in his sermon on the day of Pentecost. (Acts 3:18). Notice in the 19th verse Peter tells them to, **"Repent ye therefore, and be converted, that your sins may be blotted out, when the times of refreshing shall come from the presence of the Lord: and he shall send Jesus Christ, which before was preached unto you; whom the heaven must receive until the times of restitution of all things, which God hath spoken by the mouth of all his holy prophets since the world began."** (Acts 3:19-21).

We'll have more to say about repentance and conversion later, for the time being I want to point out two very special and important statements made in these verses. *"Times of refreshing,"* and *"Times of restitution of all things."* These two statements are connected to the second coming of Jesus Christ, at which time He shall set up the Kingdom of God here on the earth. There are so many prophecies about the second coming of the Son of Man that we could not possibly quote them all in this series without rewriting the entire bible. For this series then let us use Jesus' own words recorded in the King James version of the bible in red. Let us begin with Matthew 24:3, **"As he sat upon the Mount of Olives, the disciples came unto him privately, saying, 'tell us**

when shall these things be? And what shall be the sign of thy coming and of the end of the world?" The disciples wanted to know three things; when shall these things be? Meaning the destruction of the temple and the casting down of the stones, so that there would not be one stone upon another; What shall be the sign of thy coming? And what would be the end of the world? The very first thing that Jesus said was, **"Take heed that no man deceive you."** (Matthew 24:4). And individual, who is deceived, believes a lie. You cannot deceive one who knows the truth. For instance if you have been taught and have proven to yourself that *two + two equals four, (2 + 2 = 4)*, no amount of coaxing is going to persuade you to believe that *two + two equals seven, (2 + 2 = 7)*, because you know the truth. Jesus in his intercessory prayer for his disciples asked his Father to; **"Sanctify them through thy truth: thy word is truth."** (John 17:17). He also said to those Jews who believed on him; **"If ye continue in my word, then are ye my disciples indeed; and ye shall know the truth and the truth shall make you free. If the Son therefore shall make you free, ye shall be free indeed."** (John 8:31, 32, 36). Notice in particular his emphasis on truth and it's relationship to the word. Notice also his statement to them in the 24th chapter of Matthew as he continued to describe to them how things would be, and what they should expect at his coming, **"Heaven and earth shall pass away, but my words shall not pass away."** (verse 35).

What was some of the things that Jesus told his disciples to look for and recognize as signs of his return? Number one on the list was, **"Many shall come in my name saying, I am Christ; and shall deceive many."** Think of this statement for a moment, especially the adjective *many*. You might be tempted to look at today's world with all of it's *many* religious denominations and sects and decide, all these people who are claiming to be *born again, Holy Ghost filled, tongue talking, sanctified, and Heaven bound Christians* cannot be wrong. I want you to consider them from another perspective, since each sect or denomination claims to be the *only right one*; if their claim is true, then all the rest are *wrong or deceived*. Jesus did not say that a few would be deceived but *many*. Now notice the message, they will be proclaiming that ***Jesus is the Christ;*** they are not denying that ***He is Christ,*** the savior of the world, but yet they will deceive many. (verse 5). And then there are the others who will be proclaiming that they themselves are the Christ, and also false prophets, hear Jesus' words, **"For there shall arise false Christ's, and false prophets and shew great signs and wonders insomuch that, if it were possible, they shall deceive the very elect."** (verse 24). Only the elect will be able to discern and avoid this deception, they are the ones who shall know the truth, and as Jesus said to those Jews who believed on him, **"the truth shall make you free."**

As we stated before, it is impossible to deceive the elect, they have received the word of the ever living God and continue in it. Can you imagine the imposters, claiming that they are Christ, and performing great signs and wonders to back it up? It is no wonder that many are deceived by them. The apostle Paul warned Timothy, **"Yea, and all that would live Godly in Christ Jesus shall suffer persecution. But evil men and seducers shall wax worse and worse, deceiving and being deceived. But continue thou in the things which thou hast learned and hast been assured of, knowing of whom thou hast learned them; And from a child thou hast known the Holy Scriptures. Which are able to make thee wise unto salvation through faith which is in Christ Jesus."** (2 Timothy 3:12-15). The *Holy Scriptures*, the word of the almighty God, which Paul declares are able to *make thee wise,* so that the deceivers would not be able to get him off track. Jesus continued, **"And ye shall hear of wars and rumours of wars; see that ye be not troubled: for all these things must come to pass, but the end is not yet. For Nation shall rise against Nation, and Kingdom against Kingdom, and there shall be famines and pestilence's, and earthquakes in divers places. All these are the beginnings of sorrows. Then shall they deliver you up to be afflicted, and shall kill you: and ye shall be hated of all Nations for my name's sake. And then shall many be offended, and shall betray one another, and shall hate one another. And many false prophets shall rise, and shall deceive many. And because iniquity shall abound, the love of many shall wax cold. But he that shall endure until the end, the same shall be saved. And this gospel of the Kingdom shall be preached in all the world for a witness unto all Nations; and then shall the end come. (Matthew 24:1-14). "For then shall be great tribulations, such as was not since the beginning of the world to this time, no, nor ever shall be. And except those days should be shortened, there should no flesh be saved: but for the elect's sake those days shall be shortened.**

Then if any man shall say unto you, lo, here is Christ, or there; believe it not. For there shall arise false Christs, and false prophets, and shall shew great signs and wonders; insomuch that if it were possible, they shall deceive the very elect. Behold I have told you before. Wherefore if they shall say unto you, behold he is in the desert; go not forth; behold he is in the secret chambers; believe it not. For as the lightning cometh out of the east, and shineth even unto the west; so shall also the coming of the son of man be. For wheresoever the carcass is, there will the eagles

be gathered together. **Immediately after the tribulation of those days shall the sun be darkened, and the moon shall not give her light, and the stars shall fall from heaven, and the powers of the heavens shall be shaken; and then shall appear the sign of the Son of man in heaven: and then shall all the tribes of the earth mourn, and they shall see the Son of man coming in the clouds of heaven with power and great glory, and he shall send his angels with a great sound of a trumpet, and they shall gather his elect from the four winds, from one end of heaven to the other."** (Matthew 24:21-31). I have put special emphasis on verses 29, 30, 31, because they convey a thought commonly overlooked by many. It is commonly taught by many that the gathering away of the elect is going to be before the great tribulation, but Jesus is saying it will be immediately after. Jesus plainly tells us that this is the great tribulation, such as was not since the beginning of the world to this time, no, nor ever shall be. Whom should you believe? I believe Jesus, his words shall not pass away. Yes, He is coming again, and every eye shall see him, every living being will know that the Son of man has arrived.

Jesus spoke some very harsh words to some of today's Christians; for instance John 3:13 states, **"no man hath ascended up to heaven."** Yet millions are planning to go there; even though Jesus has already told us that *heaven and earth shall pass away.* He also inspired John to write, **"And I saw a new heaven and a new earth: for the first heaven and the first earth were passed away; and there was no more sea. And I John saw the Holy city, New Jerusalem, coming down from God out of heaven, prepared as a bride adorned for her husband. And I heard a great voice out of heaven, saying, Behold the tabernacle of God is with men and he will dwell with them, and they shall be his people, and God himself shall be with them, and be their God."** (Revelation 21:1-3). Yes, you heard right, *God himself dwelling with men, not men ascending up to heaven to dwell with God.* Can you believe and accept it?

The apostle John also wrote, **"And they sung a new song, saying, thou art worthy to take the book and to open the seals thereof: for thou wast slain, and hath redeemed us to God by thy blood out of every kindred, and tongue, and people, and nation; and hast made us unto our God kings and priests; and we shall reign on the earth."** (Revelation 5:9, 10.). Yes, on the earth, my friend the word is saying that the redeemed ones are to reign on the earth. Again I quote, **"And the seventh angel sounded: and there were great voices in heaven, saying, the kingdoms of this world are become the kingdoms of our Lord, and of his Christ; and he shall reign** forever and ever, And the four and twenty elders, which sat before God on their seats, fell upon their faces, and worshipped, saying, we give the thanks, O Lord God Almighty, which art, and wast, and art to come; because thou hast taken to thee thy great power, and hast reigned. And the nations were angry, and thy wrath is come, and the time of the dead, that they should be judged, and that thou should give reward unto thy servants the prophets, and to the saints, and them that fear thy name, small and great; and shouldest destroy them which destroy the earth." (Revelation 11:15-18.)

When we read these things in the book of Revelation we must always keep in mind that they are future prophecies, revealed to John by Jesus Christ himself, for we read at the beginning of the book; **"The revelation of Jesus Christ, which God gave unto him, to shew unto his servants things which must shortly come to pass: and he signified it by his angel unto his servant John; who bare record of the word of God and of the testimony of Jesus, and of all things that he saw."** (Revelation 1:1, 2.). I believe John's report. So it seems that, while millions have been deceived into thinking that Jesus is fixing up many mansions in heaven for them, the word is proclaiming that God is planning to *restore the earth,* (Acts 3:21), *set up his son Jesus Christ as King of kings, and Lord of lords;* (1 Timothy 6:15, Revelation 17:14), *and even dwell on the earth with men; instead of taking them to heaven to dwell with him.* (Revelation 21:1-3.) These are just a few of the prophecies proclaiming this fact, but according to Jesus and the apostle Peter all the prophets proclaimed the same thing. (Luke 24:25, 26; 2 Peter 1:19-21).

GOD'S PLAN FOR MANKIND

From what we have already read and come to understand from the direct words of Jesus himself, and the assurances of the apostle Peter, it seems to me that God intends for man to remain here on the earth. Since the prophets from the Old Testament all prophesied about the Messiah, who is Jesus; the word made flesh; (John 1:14), then they should also verify the words of Jesus and Peter. Let us take a look at some of their prophecies and see. In the book of Genesis we read the history of Abraham, the friend of God, to whom God promised the *whole world.* (Romans 4:13). But I fail to find anywhere, a promise to give him heaven or any portion thereof. In every instance where God makes a promise to Abraham and his seed, he promises him land. Let's review some of the confrontations between Abraham and the Lord. Incidentally the one referred to as the *Lord* in the Old Testament is the same one who is called the *word* in the New Testament, and who, *became flesh and dwelt among us* as Jesus. In Genesis chapter 12 we read, **"Now the Lord had said unto Abram, get thee out of thy country, and from thy kindred, and from thy father's house, unto a land that I will shew thee: and I will make of thee a great nation, and I will bless thee, and make thy name great; and thou shalt be a blessing: and I will bless them that bless thee, and curse him that curseth thee: and in thee shall all the families of the earth be blessed."** (Genesis 12:1-3). I see nothing about heaven here, although I believe that blessings come from God who's throne is in heaven. (Matthew 5:34). But the Lord does not mention anything about it to Abram at this point. Abram didn't protest making this move although he was already seventy five years old, he took his wife Sarai and his nephew Lot and departed from Haran, to go into the land of Canaan. The next time the Lord appeared unto him was after he and Lot had separated. **"And the Lord said unto Abram, after that Lot was separated from him, lift up now thine eyes, and look from the place where thou art, northward, and southward, and eastward, and westward: for all the Land which thou seest, to thee will I give it, and to thy seed forever. And I will make thy seed as the dust of the earth: so that if a man can number the dust of the earth, then shall thy seed also be numbered. Arise, walk through the land in the length of it and in the breadth of it; for I will give it unto thee."** (Genesis 13:14-17). Heaven is still not promised, the covenant is still saying *Land and posterity.* **"And behold the word of the Lord came unto him saying, this shall not be thine heir; but he that shall come forth out of thine own bowels shall be thine heir. And he brought him forth abroad; and said, look now toward heaven, and tell the stars, if thou be able to number them: and he said unto him, so shall thy seed be. And he believed in the Lord; and he counted to him for righteousness. And he said unto him, I am the Lord that brought thee out of the land of Ur of the Chaldees to give thee this Land to inherit it. In the same day the Lord made a covenant with Abram, saying, unto thy seed have I given this Land, from the river of Egypt unto the great river, the river Euphrates."** (Genesis 15:4-7, 18). Notice that the Lord is still promising Abram Land, not heaven or any part of it, but Land. You see, God made man for a specific reason, that reason is stated in Genesis chapter one verse 26; **"And God said let us make man in our image, after our likeness; and let them have dominion over the fish of the sea, and over the fowl of the air, and over the cattle, and over all the earth, and over every creeping thing that creepeth upon the earth."** That is why God made man, *to have dominion over the earth.* But man has allowed himself to be persuaded that his place is in heaven with God. His every effort is to get away from the earth and go to heaven. Man does not want to accept the fact that God is the potter and man is the clay. (Genesis 2:7). God determines everything, and I do mean everything, including the boundaries of man's habitation. (Acts 17:26). More about Abram and the covenant; **"And when Abram was ninety years old and nine, the Lord appeared unto Abram and said unto him, I am the almighty God, walk before me and be thou perfect. And I will make my covenant between me and thee, and I will multiply thee exceedingly. And Abram fell on his face, and God talked with him, saying, As for me, behold my covenant is with thee, and thou shalt be a father of many nations. Neither shall thy name any more be called Abram, but thy name shall be Abraham; for a father of many nations have I made thee. And I will make thee exceeding fruitful, and I will make nations of thee, and kings shall come out of thee. And I will establish my covenant between me and thee and thy seed after thee in their generations for an everlasting covenant, to be a God unto thee, and thy seed, after thee. And I will give unto thee, and to thy seed after thee, the Land wherein thou art a stranger, all the Land of Canaan, for an everlasting possession; and I will be their God."** (Genesis 17:1-8).

You must remember one thing about God; He does not change. He created man for a specific reason. He has not changed his mind, man will yet fulfill God's will for him. God boasts through the prophet Isaiah; **"Remember the former things of old: for I am God, and there is none else; I am God, and there is none like me. Declaring the end from the beginning, and from ancient times the things that are not yet done, saying, my council shall stand, and I will do all my pleasure; calling a ravenous bird from the east, the man that executed my council from a far country; yea, I have spoken it, I will also bring it to pass; I have proposed it, I will also do it."** (Isaiah 46:9-11). And what did God propose? Again I repeat from Genesis 1:26b; **"And let them have dominion over the fish of the sea, and over the fowl of the air, and over the cattle, and over all the earth and over every creeping thing that creepeth upon the earth."** God has not forgotten, he remembered it through David; **"What is man that thou art mindful of him? and the son of man that thou visiteth him? For thou hast made him a little lower than the angels, and hast crowned him with glory and honour. Thou madest him to have dominion over the works of thy hands: thou hast put all things under his feet; all sheep and oxen, yea, and the beasts of the field; the fowl of the air, and the fish of the sea, and whatsoever passeth through the paths of the seas. O, Lord our Lord, how excellent is** thy name in all the earth." (Psalm 8:4-9). The great creator God has already purposed man's destiny, and it does not include going to heaven I am sorry to say, and I am sure many are going to be disappointed when they search the scriptures, and find that they no where promise heaven as a reward for the redeemed of the Lord. As I continue with this series, it becomes more and more apparent to me why I was led of the Spirit to begin at the sixth chapter of the book of Matthew verse ten, *"Thy Kingdom come, thy will be done in earth as it is in heaven."*

When you study the scriptures, both old and new testaments, it becomes obvious that God's intentions for man was to have him rule the earth, and everything that he had put upon it, including the seas and everything in them, and the air and everything in it. But, it seems that man is determined that he will go up to heaven. Notice some of his popular songs; *"Going up yonder to be with my Lord,"* another proclaims, *"When we all get to heaven,"* and still another says, *"Heaven is my goal."* I am reminded at this point of another being that decided that he would go up and take over God's throne; notice the following scriptures; **"How art thou fallen from heaven, O Lucifer, son of the morning! How art thou cut down to the ground, which didst weaken the nations! For thou hast said in thine heart, I will ascend into heaven, I will sit also upon the mount of the congregation, in the sides of the north: I will ascend above the heights of the clouds, I will be like the Most High. Yet thou shalt be brought down to hell, to the sides of the pit."** (Isaiah 14:12-15; Luke 10:18; Revelation 12:8, 9). This being was none other than Satan, who was cast down. He, like many of mankind, does not want to fulfill the destiny which God has planned for him, but instead, he wants to choose his own. See also Ezekiel 28:12-15.

GOD WILL DWELL WITH MEN

Even after God had driven the man out of the Garden of Eden, he made known his desire to dwell with men to Moses, notice; **"And let them make me a sanctuary; that I may dwell among them."** (Exodus 25:8). God will do his pleasure, no one can prevent him. He is supreme and he changeth not. Even though the first man Adam allowed Satan to rob him of his fellowship with God there in the garden, the great creator God, sent forth another man, the man Jesus, to *"restore all things."* Read all about this man Jesus and his accomplishments in the book of Hebrews. Hear it's beginning; **"God, who at sundry times and in divers manners spake in times past unto the fathers by the prophets, hath in these last days spoken unto us** by his son, whom he hath appointed heir of all things, by whom also he made the worlds; who being the brightness of his glory, and the express image of his person, and upholding all things by the word of his power, when he had by himself purged our sins, sat down on the right hand of the majesty on high; Being made so much better than the angels, as he hath by inheritance obtained a more excellent name than they. For unto which of the angels said he at any time, thou art my son, this day have I begotten thee? And again, when he bringeth in the first begotten into the world, he saith, And let all the angels of God worship him. And of the angels he saith, who maketh his angel's spirits, and his ministers a flame of fire. But unto the son he saith, thy throne O, God, is forever and ever; a scepter of righteousness is the scepter of thy kingdom." (Hebrews 1:1-8). Yes, my friend, Jesus has come in the flesh, overcome the world, and the prince of this present world, Satan; and has sat down on the right hand of the Majesty on high, *awaiting the times of the restitution of all things.* Don't be deceived, my friend, *Jesus is coming again* to this earth. He will *restore all things.* He has *already paid the price for our redemption,* he will *establish the kingdom of God on the earth, and sit on it, and reign forever and ever, as the King of kings, and Lord of lords.*

Yes it is true, Jesus said it, I believe, and that settles it. God himself shall make his abode in the city, the New Jerusalem, and shall be our God, and we shall be his people. *Hear the declarations of the Lord Jesus Christ, of the revelations which God gave unto him, to shew unto his servants things which must shortly come to pass;* "And I saw a new heaven and a new earth; for the first heaven and the first earth were passed away; and there was no more sea. And I John saw the Holy City, New Jerusalem, coming down from God out of heaven, prepared as a bride adorned for her husband. And I heard a great voice out of heaven saying, Behold the Tabernacle of God is with men, and he will dwell with them, and they shall be his people, and God himself shall be with them, and be their God. And God shall wipe away all tears from their eyes; and there shall be no more death, neither sorrow, nor crying, neither shall there be any more pain: for the former things are passed away. And he that sat upon the throne said, Behold I make all things new. And he said unto me, write; for these words are true and faithful. And he said unto me, it is done. I am alpha and omega, the beginning and the end. I will give unto him that is athirst of the fountain of the waters of life freely. He that over cometh shall inherit all things; and I will be his God, and he shall be my son. But the fearful, and unbelieving, and the abominable, and murderers, and whoremongers, and sorcerers, and idolaters, and all liars, shall have their part in the lake which burneth with fire and brimstone: which is the second death." (Revelation 21:1-8). It is no mystery to me now why I was lead to begin this segment with what is commonly called the Lord's prayer. Jesus is telling his disciples to *pray for God's kingdom to come. Pray that the will of God be done on earth as it is in heaven.* I wonder do you have any idea what the fulfillment of these two phrases would do for our earth today, should they come to pass. Go back and read Revelation 21:4-7 again, just for starters.

BEYOND HUMAN IMAGINATION

The human mind cannot see the changes that the Almighty God will make in the earth without Spiritual revelation. Just as John was in the Spirit on the Lord's Day when he was shown all these, **"things which must shortly come to pass"** so the reader must also be in the Spirit in order to understand these things.

The changes that take place are astounding. I shall not try to reiterate them all in this writing, but I am urged to point out just a few of them. I will start off with the phrase, **"and God himself shall be with them, and be their God."** (Revelation 21:3b). Just imagine being able to walk and talk with God himself just as you walk and talk with your friend's today. Look him in the face just as you would any other person. Just picture the earth, with all of it's billions of people, and nobody *crying*, nobody *dying*, nobody *sorrowful*, no *pain and suffering*, all these things having been *done away with*. Can you believe it? Perhaps it is difficult for you, but I believe it. God revealed it to his son Jesus Christ, Jesus Christ revealed it to his servant John, and told him to write it in a book. The book has come all the way down through many generations to us today. I believe John's report, and that settles it for me. I am convinced that this word is the word of the all wise; ever living, all powerful, creator God who is able to make his will known to us. Able to cause men to write what he wants written, the way he wants it written, and preserve it, and present it to the world he created. So, not only do I have John's report, but I also have the word from the **"mouth of all the Holy Prophets since the world began."** How about you my friend? *Do you now believe?* All the events that have taken place in the world since Adam was driven out of the Garden of Eden, have been designed to bring about God's original purpose. He has not changed his mind about one single thing. Jesus will surely come again. When? God has not yet revealed the time, but his promises are sure. Jesus gave us the signs by which we can know when the time is near. Many of them have already come to pass, but there are yet many more that must be fulfilled. He warned us to watch and pray, so that day will not come upon us unawares; Notice: **"So likewise ye, when ye see these things come to pass, know ye that the kingdom of God is nigh at hand. Verily I say unto you, this generation shall not pass away, till all be fulfilled. Heaven and earth shall pass away; but my words shall not pass away. And take heed to yourselves, lest at any time your hearts be overcharged with surfeiting, and drunkenness, and care of this life, and so that day come upon you unawares. For as a snare shall it come on all them that dwell on the face of the whole earth. Watch ye therefore, and pray always, that ye may be accounted worthy to escape all these things that shall come to pass, and to stand before the Son of Man."** (Luke 21:31-36).

We can be ready for his coming, friend, all we have to do is work the works of God. Do you want to know what the works of God are? Let Jesus tell you: **"Then said they unto him, what shall we do that we might work the works of God? Jesus answered and said unto them, this is the work of God, that ye believe on him whom he hath sent."** (John 6:28, 29). Perhaps this sounds to simple to you, especially, after all you have probably heard from many crusaders, who have informed you that you must do this, and you must do that; don't believe them, believe the Lord Jesus Christ. He is the one whom God has sent; he is the one whom God the Father hath sealed, it is through him that the world will be saved. Believe him and receive eternal life, there is no other way, there is no other work; **"For by grace are ye saved through faith; and that not of yourselves; it is the gift of God: not of works lest any man should boast."** (Ephesians 2:8, 9). Believe and receive.

CHAPTER 5

Jesus Was Born Again

You may not have heard that statement before: but before you form any conclusions I would like to refer back to a statement made earlier in these writings, in which I quoted from Acts 3:19; to wit, **"Repent ye therefore and be *converted*, that your sins may be blotted out, when the times of refreshing shall come from the presence of the Lord."** I have italicized the word *converted* here because many today would have used the word *born again* instead of *converted,* and it is this misuse of the *born again phrase* that has deceived many and even today cause many to labor under false illusions.

We must remember that the apostle Peter spoke these words at a time when he was filled with the Holy Spirit, and his words were carefully chosen so that all might understand and come into the knowledge of the truth. We must first be converted. We are later born again into the kingdom of God as his sons. There are millions today who are shouting to the housetops, *"I know I have been born again,"* or *"I am a born again Christian."* But we need to search the scriptures and accept the word of the *Holy Scriptures.* When we do this then we will know where we stand; instead of listening to some man or woman whom the enemy has deceived, and becoming deceived along with them. The apostle Paul wrote to Timothy; *"From a child thou hast known the holy scriptures, which are able to make thee wise unto salvation through faith which is in Christ Jesus."* (2 Timothy 3:15). Let us look at some scriptures concerning this subject of rebirth and compare them with the life of Jesus, and our own lives as well. The very first time this phrase is used in the new testament is in John 3:3; **"Jesus answered and said unto him, verily, verily, I say unto thee, except a man be born again, he cannot see the kingdom of God. Nicodemus saith unto him, how can a man be born when he is old? Can he enter the second time into his mother's womb and be born? Jesus answered, verily, verily, I say unto thee, except a man be born of water and of the Spirit, he cannot enter into the kingdom of God. That** which is born of the flesh is flesh: and that which is born of the Spirit is spirit. Marvel not that I said unto thee, ye must be born again. The wind bloweth where it listeth, and thou heareth the sound thereof, but canst not tell whence it cometh, and whither it goeth; so is everyone that is born of the Spirit. Nicodemus answered and said unto him, how can these things be? (John 3:3-9).

This was a very valid question from Nicodemus' point of view. How can these things be? One might ask, what things? Let us examine this conversation very closely. This condition of which Jesus spoke (*born again)* is necessary for a man to be able to *see the kingdom of God,* let alone enter into it, or participate in it. Nicodemus knew and understood that returning to his mother's womb was out of the question, a physical impossibility. And he also knew that this man whom he had come to by night, perhaps because he was afraid or ashamed to be seen with him in public; was nobody's fool or crackpot. Out of sheer curiosity he asked the question; *how can a man be born when he is old?*

Jesus proceeded to reveal a truth to Nicodemus that many have not understood to this very day. Note these words; **"except a man be born of water and of the Spirit he cannot enter into the kingdom of God."** Two different births are spoken of here, born of water is the first. Many of us are familiar with the water birth, many times I have heard women and doctors speak of the water birth. They say that unless the water breaks the child will be stillborn, or dead. Such a child will never see life as we know it. If a child does not enter into this present life, which is the first birth, and I might add, the one that Nicodemus was familiar with; he certainly cannot enter into the second birth of which Jesus spoke. Since at least two births are necessary (*you cannot be born again until you are born the first time)* for a man to enter into the kingdom of God; and since Jesus was a man, born of a woman, it was absolutely necessary for him to be born again according to his own words. This fact is plainly revealed by the scriptures as we shall see.

Notice the apostle Paul's writings to the Colossians chapter 1:12-23. **"Giving thanks unto the father, which hath made us meet to be partakers of the inheritance of the saints in light: who hath delivered us from the power of darkness, and hath translated us into the kingdom of his dear son: in whom we have redemption through his blood, even the forgiveness of sins: who is the image of the invisible God, the *firstborn of every creature*: For by him were all things created, that are in heaven, and that are in earth, visible and invisible, whether they be thrones, or dominions, or principalities, or powers: all things were created by him, and for him; And he is before all things, and by him all things consist.**

And he is the head of the body, the Church: who is the beginning, the *firstborn from the dead;* that in all things he might have the preeminence. For it pleased the Father that in him should all fullness dwell; And having made peace through the blood of his cross, by him to reconcile all things unto himself; by him, I say, whether they be things in earth, or things in heaven. And you that were sometimes alienated and enemies in your mind by wicked works, yet now hath he reconciled. In the body of his flesh through death, to present you holy and unblameable and unreproveable in his sight: *If ye continue in the faith grounded and settled, and be not moved away from the hope of the gospel,* which ye have heard, and which was preached to every creature which is under heaven; whereof I Paul am made a minister."

There are some key phrases in this quotation that I would like to have you take a very close look at. Note verse 15, **"Who is the image of the invisible God, the *firstborn of every creature."*** We see Jesus here as *the firstborn of every creature,* remember firstborn. Again in verse 18; **"and he is the head of the body, the church: who is the beginning, the *firstborn from the dead*; that in all things he might have the preeminence."** I keep repeating this word *firstborn* for one reason, so that you might recognize the depth of this statement. Jesus Christ is the firstborn of every creature without exception. Not even the angels can lay claim to this honor, for you see angels were not born into the kingdom of God; they were created. Notice, **"Who maketh his angels Spirits."** (Hebrews 1:7). Yes angels are spirits, but they were created so by God, but listen to the apostle Paul's description of Jesus in Hebrews chapter 1; **"God who at sundry times and in divers manners spake in times past unto the fathers by the prophets, Hath in these last days spoken unto us by his son, whom he hath appointed heir of all things, by whom also he made the worlds; Who being the brightness of his glory, and the express image of his person, and upholding all things by the word of his power, when he had by himself purged our sins, sat down on the right hand of the majesty on high; Being made so much better than the angels, as he hath by inheritance obtained a more excellent name than they. For unto which of the angels said he at any time, Thou art my son, this day have I begotten thee? And again, I will be to him a father, and he shall be to me a son."** (verses 1-5). He continues in verse 9, **"Thou hast loved righteousness and hated iniquity: therefore God, even thy God, hath anointed thee with the oil of gladness above thy fellows. But to which of the angels said he at any time, sit on my right hand, until I make thine enemies thy footstool?** (verses 9, 13).

Jesus has been elevated above all by becoming the first to enter the kingdom of God by Spiritual birth, and has been given a name that is above every name. Yes my friend, ***Jesus was born of the Spirit,*** just as he informed Nicodemus that everyone that enters the Kingdom of God must be. I continue with the apostle Paul's writings to the Romans, **"And we know that all things work together for good to them that love God, to them who are the called according to his purpose. For whom he did foreknow, he also did predestinate to be conformed to the image of his son, that he might be the *firstborn* of many brethren."** (Romans 8:28, 29). Notice that word *firstborn;* see if you can get the connection.

Jesus himself stated; **"I am the way, the truth, and the life, no man cometh unto the Father but by me."** (John 14:6). **"Verily, verily, I say unto you, I am the door of the sheep. All that ever came before me are thieves and robbers: but the sheep did not hear them. I am the door; by me if any man enter in, he shall be saved and shall go in and out and find pasture."** (John10:7-9). A door is an entranceway to some place, or something, in this case the door leads to everlasting life. Jesus entered, through the resurrection from the dead, and a change. (John 20:17). Since this is the way that man may enter into the Kingdom of God, *(I might also add that it is the only way),* and since Jesus was the first to do so, he is therefore called the firstborn, but the scripture implies that there will be many, notice the phrase, firstborn of many brethren. The apostle Paul tells us about this in his letter to the church of God at Corinth, I quote; **"Behold I shew you a mystery; we shall not all sleep, (die) but we shall all be changed, in a moment, in the twinkling of an eye, at the last trump: for the trumpet shall sound, and the dead shall be raised incorruptible, and we shall be changed."** Can you grasp this fact? Jesus was the first to partake of his doctrine, first preached to Nicodemus. Jesus answered to Nicodemus, **"Verily, verily, I say unto thee, except a man be born again, he cannot see the Kingdom of God."** (John 3:3). Nicodemus did not get the point, so don't feel bad if you have not come to understand what Jesus meant. Even after Jesus explained to Nicodemus, he still did not understand, listen to his response. **"Nicodemus saith unto him, how can a man be born when he is old? Can he enter a second time into his mother's womb and be born? Jesus answered, Verily, verily, I say unto thee, except a man be born of water and of the Spirit he cannot enter into the Kingdom of God. That which is born of the flesh is flesh; and that which is born of the Spirit is spirit. Marvel not that I said unto thee ye must be born again."** (John 3:4-7). Nicodemus still didn't understand, verse 9, just as many today do not yet understand the rebirth Jesus spoke of to Nicodemus. Many strive to make something of Jesus statement that he had not intended.

Jesus said to Nicodemus, ***marvel not***: that is to say, don't be upset because I said to you, you must be born again. Some believe and teach that being baptized and receiving the Holy Ghost, constitutes rebirth, but note what Jesus said to Nicodemus**, "that which is born of the flesh is flesh."** Even though a man is born of water, that is the common human birth, he must also be born of the Spirit. (see 1 Corinthians 15:46-49). Jesus was first born of Mary, a fleshly human birth; and then he was born of the Spirit, (raised or brought forth from death and the grave, and changed, by the Spirit; becoming the firstborn from the dead. (Colossians 1:18). Here then is the real test of being born again; Jesus said to Nicodemus, **"The wind bloweth where it listeth, and thou heareth the sound thereof, but canst not tell whence it cometh, and whither it goeth; so is everyone that is born of the Spirit."** (John 3:8). Can you accept what Jesus is saying to Nicodemus? Listen, anyone born of the Spirit is like the wind, you don't see the wind, you just hear it whistling through the trees, or you see flags and leaves being moved by it, but you cannot tell where it came from or where it goes. What many today call born again is what the apostles called converted. On the day of Pentecost the apostle Peter told the congregation, **"Repent, and be baptized everyone of you in the name of Jesus Christ for the remission of sins, and ye shall receive the gift of the Holy Ghost."** (Acts 2:38). I believe it is significant to note that the apostle Peter did not say repent and be born again. Peter, because of his own conversion knew that receiving the Holy Ghost is to become impregnated with the very Spirit of God, not yet born, but similar to a woman who is impregnated by a man. The child is not yet born, but is being formed in the womb. After the period of gestation, usually nine months, the woman then give birth to a child. The child is not yet born until it comes forth from the womb of the mother. Let us compare this thought with the life of Jesus. At the river of Jordan, when Jesus persuaded John to baptize him something very interesting took place. It is recorded in the last three verses of Matthew chapter 3 and I quote; **"And Jesus answering saith unto him, suffer it to be so now: for thus it becometh us to fulfill all righteousness. Then he suffered him. And Jesus when he was baptized, went up straightway out of the water: and lo, the heavens were opened unto him, and he saw the Spirit of God descending like a dove, and lighting upon him. And lo, a voice from heaven, saying, this is my beloved Son in whom I am well pleased."**

This was Matthew's account, let us read Mark's account of this same incident. **"And it came to pass in those days that Jesus came from Nazareth** of Galilee, and was baptized of John in Jordan. And straightway coming up out of the water, he saw the heavens opened, and the Spirit like a dove descending upon him: and there came a voice from heaven, saying, thou art my beloved son, in whom I am well pleased." (Mark 1:9-11.) Luke records; "Now when all the people were baptized, it came to pass that Jesus also being baptized, and praying, the heaven was opened, and the Holy Ghost descended in a bodily shape like a dove upon him, and a voice came from heaven, which said, Thou art my beloved Son; in thee I am well pleased." (Luke 3:21, 22). All three seem to agree on one thing, that is, the descending of the **"Spirit like a dove."** Yes Jesus received the *Holy Spirit*, just as Peter told his hearers on the day of Pentecost that they would receive, if they repented and were baptized for the remission of sins. This **Spirit** would remain in him until the **third day** of his death and would *quicken his mortal body,* causing him to *come alive again*, thus making him the first ever to be so raised, and changed.

Hear the apostle Paul's declaration to the Romans; **"If the Spirit of him that raised up Jesus from the dead dwell in you, he that raised up Christ from the dead shall also quicken your mortal body by his Spirit that dwelleth in you."** (Romans 8:11.) The change is evident from John's testimony of the resurrection of Jesus in chapter 20; especially the discourse with Mary Magdalene. Notice, **"Then the disciples went away unto their own home. But Mary stood without at the sepulcher weeping: and as she wept, she stooped down, and looked into the sepulcher, and seeth two angels in white sitting the one at the head, and the other at the feet, where the body of Jesus had lain. And they say unto her, woman why weepeth thou? She saith unto them, because they have taken away my Lord and I know not where they have laid him, and when she had thus said she turned herself back, and saw Jesus standing, and knew not that it was Jesus. Jesus saith unto her, woman why weepeth thou? Whom seeketh thou? She, supposing him to be the gardener, saith unto him, sir, if thou have born him hence, tell me where thou hast laid him, and I will take him away. Jesus saith unto her, Mary. She turned herself and saith unto him, Rabboni: which is to say, Master. Jesus saith unto her, touch me not for I am not yet ascended to my Father, but go to my brethren, and say unto them, I ascend unto my Father, and your Father; and to my God and your God."** (John 20:10-17.) Notice the phrase, *"touch me not."* Jesus forbade her to touch him, it could be that he was being changed from mortal to immortal. It is evident that he was *changed* after this account with Mary, for later that same day he stood in the midst of the disciples and showed them his hands and his side, he even invited them to touch him. He later invited Thomas to examine *the nail prints in his hands, and thrust his hand into his side.* (John 20:27, 28).

He even invited them to handle him; notice, **"And as they thus spake, Jesus himself stood in the midst of them, and saith unto them, peace be unto you. But they were terrified and affrighted, and supposed that they had seen a spirit. And he said unto them, why are ye troubled? And why do thoughts arise in your hearts? Behold my hands and my feet, that it is I myself, handle me and see; for a spirit hath not flesh and bones as ye see me have."** (Luke 24:36-39.) Flesh and bones; no mention of blood, this is indeed a change to note, an indication of what Jesus had said to Nicodemus, **"That which is born of Spirit is Spirit."** (John 3:6). Jesus was now able to appear and disappear at will. (Luke 24:31, 36, 51). Jesus had now been *born of the Spirit.* (Acts 1:9-11). As believers we must guard against false teachers; Jesus called them thieves and robbers, who would have you try to get into the kingdom some other way than through a resurrection and change as he did. How else would you explain his being called the **"firstborn among many brethren."** (Romans 8:29.) How else could he be called the **"firstborn from the dead."** (Colossians 1:18.) There had been other resurrections prior to that of Jesus: for instance, there was the son of the Shunammite woman whom Elisha restored to life; but he died again later. (2 Kings 4:32-37). Then there was the son of the widow of Nain whom Jesus himself raised from the dead, but he later died. (Luke 7:11-15.) Jesus also raised up Lazarus who had been dead four days, and even though Jesus loved Lazarus and his sisters Mary and Martha, Lazarus later died again. (John 11:43, 44.) The apostle Peter prayed and commanded Dorcas to arise, and she awakened from the dead, but she later died again. (Acts 9:36-43). All these incidents had one thing in common, those resurrected had their bodies made alive again by the restoration of the flow of blood through their veins. The scripture tells that the *life of the flesh is in the blood.* (Leviticus 17:10-14; Deuteronomy 12:23.) Jesus had no blood after his resurrection from the dead. He no longer depended upon the flow of blood through his body for life. No other man or being has gone through this process, before or after Jesus. Jesus is unique; to this very day no other being has entered into eternal life, or into the presence of the Father, through a resurrection from the dead, except Jesus.

There will be an *innumerable company* that will follow, that is why he is called **"the firstborn among many brethren."** That is also why believers are called **"joint heirs with Christ."** (Romans 8:17.) Jesus warned his disciples, **"Take heed that no man deceive you"** (Matthew 24:4.) Peter warned of "**cunningly devised fables**" (2 Peter 1:16.) Today our world is filled with deceptions and fables. For anyone to think that he or she can enter into the kingdom of God any other way than that provided through Jesus, makes them a "**thief and robber.**" For anyone to think that they have already been *born again* (*born of the Spirit*) without having gone through the resurrection or a change is to be deceived. Yes, my friend, I am glad that Jesus has already been born again of the Spirit, paving the way for as many as will receive him, to be born into the Kingdom of God, by a resurrection from the dead and or a change. *Do you now believe?* Listen to this declaration from the gospel according to John, "**For God sent not his son into the world to condemn the world; but that the world through him might be saved. He that believeth on him is not condemned: but he that believeth not is condemned already, because he hath not believed in the name of the only begotten Son of God.**" (John3:17, 18.) My dear friend, *believing* is what it is all about. God is not a respecter of persons, he will save all who believe on his Son. Believe on him today and receive everlasting life.

CHAPTER 6

A New Heaven and A New Earth

When you look at our world today with all of it's joys and sorrows, it is no wonder that mankind has fallen prey to Satan's idea of going up to heaven. Especially since there are so few joys to be had, and sorrows seem to be without end. Ask almost any member of any church today and they will tell you that they are on their way to heaven. Jehovah's Witnesses are mostly excepted. They are saying that only one hundred and forty four thousand are destined to go to heaven. I am forced to admit that the prospect of going to heaven is ideal, if we could bring it to pass. Just the idea of having to spend eternity here on this earth with all it's problems is enough to cause one to desire a better place. Here you struggle for forty years trying to acquire a home that you can call your own, and when you finally make that last mortgage payment you give a sigh of relief. Now you can take it easy; or so you think; no more mortgage payments to make. You have not only paid off that thirty-year debt, but you also managed to save a good sum to retire on. You have acquired a brand new car, your closet contains almost anything that you would want to wear. You are considered to be one of the well-to-do people in your neighborhood, you are well thought of in your church congregation, you're not really old at sixty years. Only about five more years to go before retirement. Then you report for work one morning and find that the company is downsizing because of the failing economy. One of the employees caught up in the layoff is you. At age sixty it will be difficult to find work. Beside the age factor, your health has begun to fail, the visits to the doctor and the hospital have become more frequent. Your being out of work does not in any way curtail the rising prices of goods and services. Your unemployment compensation will only hold you for a little while. At the end of your compensation you will still be several years away from retirement age. Then you will have to rely on your savings. I could go on and on with the possible situations that could come up in this present world so that an individual would desire to pack up and go to some other place and leave all the sorrows and miseries behind.

We have pointed out a number of things that can occur in our lives here on the earth, but there are a number of things that we did not mention in the scenario previously presented. Let us dwell with this situation a little longer for clarity sake. In spite of all the problems and difficulties that confront us here on the earth I have yet to confront a human being, or any other living being for that matter that wants to die in order to get away from the earth. Everything that I have confronted, that is living, wants to continue living. That goes for the smallest insect to the largest mammal. The strange thing about the human element on earth is that everybody wants to go to heaven but nobody wants to die. This tells me that nobody is absolutely sure that they are going to heaven when they die. If they were I'm sure they would be lined up for miles looking for their opportunity to leave this earth and go to their new home in heaven. Just coming face to face with this situation caused me to start taking inventory of what is available to mankind right here on this earth. Do you know that I have been unable to come up with one single thing that mankind needs or wants that is not already available to him. I was really surprised when I began to take inventory of the various needs, wants, and desires of mankind, and not only mankind, but every creature great and small that our Father has put here on the earth. When I read Genesis chapter one and two again I was reassured that God had not left out one single thing that was necessary for the existence of his creatures. Have you ever considered our world from this point of view? I even asked my wife to try and think of something that she wanted, needed, or desired, that is not available in our present world. Her answer was rather comical; she said, *"some one to buy me a mansion and a Cadillac and give me a few million dollars to keep them up."* This is how most people look at things around them. Strangely enough I could not think of one single thing that I need, want, or desire, that is not already here on this planet earth. Not even one. How about you, can you think of something that you need, want, or desire that God in his wisdom has not provided? What is it then that makes man so dead set on getting away from the earth? When we read God's purpose for making man, revealed in Genesis, and the provisions he made for his well being and comfort, you wonder why he cannot be at peace on the earth along with his fellowman and the other creatures that God gave him dominion over. I have been a resident on this earth for well over seventy years at this writing, and I have seen mankind go from horse and buggy to jet airliner. From a five mile-an-hour pace walking, to well over fifteen-hundred miles per hour in a modern jet plane. I have witnessed mankind's progress from communicating by pony express to modern day telecommunications, where we are able to carry on a dialogue with someone half-a-world away while watching their facial expressions on television. The things that the creator has revealed unto man are simply astounding, but yet mankind is still unsatisfied with his place and surroundings. Nothing seems to make him content.

Thus it is very easy for the enemy to pawn off on an individual the idea of going up to heaven. Didn't Jesus say that he was going to prepare a place for you? And when he left didn't he ascend up to heaven? Well then, if he went to heaven to prepare a place for us believers, doesn't that mean that we are to go there to be with him? Sounds logical enough, just logical enough for someone who has not searched the scriptures to be deceived by it. I would like to point out a few things that shouldn't be difficult for any person to understand. First of all let's really hear what Jesus said; for this we will go to John 14: beginning at verse one I quote: **"Let not your heart be troubled, ye believe in God, believe also in me.** (there's that word believe again). **In my Father's house are many mansions: If it were not so, I would have told you. I go to prepare a place for you."** *Did you get what he said?* I repeat, **"I go to prepare a place for you."** I humbly submit; the heaven to which Jesus ascended is already prepared, there is nothing missing or out of place there. The dwelling place of the Most High is perfect, so it is not likely that he was talking about preparing or fixing up a place for us there.

A mansion is not a mansion unless it is prepared to be a mansion. Jesus said they were already there *in his Father's house.* What ever, or where ever the place is that Jesus spoke of, it was not yet ready at the time of his departure. Quoting again from John 14:3, **"And if I go and prepare a place for you, I will come again, and receive you unto myself, that where I am, there ye may be also."** Notice, he did not say anything about *taking you any place,* the phrase is *receive you,* and, *where I am there ye may be also.* Now you need to make sure that you read this statement correctly, ***not adding anything,*** or ***taking anything away.*** If Jesus goes away and comes back again, I ask you where will he be when he gets back? ***Answer; on the earth.*** Again I ask you to note that he did not say anything about ***taking you anyplace, but receive you unto myself.*** I truly hope that you can receive this message from the mouth of Jesus himself. Let us listen to the apostle John describe the destiny of those redeemed by the blood of the lamb, who is Jesus, (John 1:29). **"And I beheld, and lo, in the midst of the throne and of the four beasts, and in the midst of the Elders, stood a lamb as it had been slain, having seven horns and seven eyes, which are the seven Spirits of God sent forth into all the earth. And he came and took the book out of the right hand of him that sat upon the throne. And when he had taken the book, the four** beasts and four and twenty Elders fell down before the Lamb, having every one of them harps, and golden vials full of odours, which are the prayers of saints. And they sung a new song, saying, Thou art worth to take the book, and to open the seals thereof: for thou wast slain, and hast redeemed us to God by thy blood out of every kindred, and tongue, and people, and nation: and hast made us unto our God kings and priests; and we shall reign on the earth." (Revelation 5:6-10.)

It would appear from these scriptures that our God has already determined what he would have those for whom he gave his only begotten Son to do. Listen to John again; **"And the seventh angel sounded, and there were great voices in heaven, saying, the kingdoms of this world are become the kingdoms of our Lord and his Christ; and he shall reign forever and ever."** (Revelation 11:15.) From these scriptures I am led to believe that *Jesus himself is going to take over the kingdoms of this world and rule them forever after.* Can you receive these plainly stated facts from your bible and believe them? I can. You see there are none of our problems in heaven, no, not one.

Heaven is another realm, or dimension of existence altogether different from ours. Heaven is an ideal place, it is a place to be desired by all. No growing old and useless, no screaming sirens in the middle of the night as emergency vehicles rush someone to the hospital. No funeral processions holding up traffic as the dead are carried to their final resting place; in fact there is no dying there, so there is no need for undertakers, cemeteries, or processions to them. For those who abide there, *peace, love, joy, and everlasting life in the presence of the great creator God is without end.* Certainly this present world in it's present condition leaves a lot to be desired. Listen to Job as he describes the plight of man on this present earth. **"Man that is born of a woman is of few days and full of trouble. He cometh forth like a flower and is cut down; he fleeth also as a shadow, and continueth not."** (Job 14:1, 2). Yes Job says that a man that is born of a woman is short lived, and the few days that he has are filled with trouble. Just like a flower cut to form a bouquet, when it blooms out in it's prime, so a man is cut off in his prime. Just when he is beginning to learn what living is all about, he dies and does not continue. Job continues, **"Seeing his days are determined, the number of his months are with thee, thou hast appointed his bounds that he cannot pass. For there is hope of a tree, if it be cut down, that it will sprout again, and that the tender branch thereof will not cease. But man dieth and wasteth away; yea, man giveth up the ghost, and where is he? As the waters fail from the sea, and the flood decayeth and drieth up: so** man lieth down, and riseth not; till the heavens be no more, they shall not awake, nor be raised out of their sleep. O that thou wouldest hide me in the grave, that thou wouldest keep me secret, until thy wrath be past, that thou wouldest appoint me a set time, and remember me! If a man die, shall he live again? All the days of my appointed time will I wait, till my change come. Thou shalt call, and I will answer thee; thou wilt have a desire to the work of thine hands.** (Job 14:5, 7, 10-15.)

God had said to the man, **"cursed is the ground for thy sake, in sorrow shalt thou eat of it all the days of thy life; Thorns and thistles shall it bring forth to thee; and thou shalt eat the herb of the field; in the sweat of thy face shalt thou eat bread, till thou return unto the ground; for out of it wast thou taken; for dust thou art, and unto dust shalt thou return."** (Genesis 3:17b-19.) In view of these statements and the everyday facts of life that we experience, it is not difficult to understand man's desire to *get away from the earth, and go up to heaven.* It would seem that we are doomed to suffer all of the things that Job refers to as long as we are on this earth. But I think that most people who read John 14 fail to get the full impact of Jesus statement, **"I will come again."** We need to take him at his word instead of trying to figure out what he meant, Jesus meant just what he said. While many will be looking for Jesus to come and *pick them up, so to speak, and take them away,* the scripture is saying that **Jesus will be coming to take over and rule the whole earth.** Those whom he *receive unto himself* will rule with him. It is interesting to note that the scripture never indicates that the Saints are being taken up to heaven to *possess it,* but all through the scriptures they plainly state that *the inheritance of the Saints is land and the, "Kingdom of Heaven."* (See Matthew 5:3, 5, 10.)

The scripture records the words, *"Kingdom of Heaven"* and many have assumed that the kingdom of which Jesus spoke is in heaven, and that those who are to possess it are going to go there to possess it. This is not necessarily so, you need to note that the phrase is, *"Kingdom of Heaven"* not, *"Kingdom in Heaven."* There is a whole world of difference in these two statements. Perhaps a brief look at the prophecies of Daniel will serve to enlighten the situation a bit. You see the final world ruling empire will be the, *"Kingdom of Heaven."* (Daniel 2:44, 7:13, 14.) *The final world ruling King will be Jesus Christ.* (Revelation 19:11-16.) Daniel saw Jesus Christ, the son of man, as he ascended up to his father on a cloud. Notice how Jesus departed from this earth as seen by the apostles; **"And when he had spoken these things, while they beheld, he was taken up, and a cloud received him out of their sight. And while they looked steadfastly toward heaven as he went** up, behold, two men stood by them in white apparel; which also said, ye men of Galilee, why stand ye gazing up into heaven? This same Jesus, which is taken up from you into heaven, shall so come in like manner as ye have seen him go into heaven." (Acts 1:9-11.)

Where did Jesus go? Let us allow the prophet Daniel to take over at this point. **"I saw in the night visions, and behold, one like the son of man came with the clouds of heaven, and came to the ancient of days, and they brought him near before him. And there was given him dominion, and glory, and a kingdom, that all people, nations and languages, should serve him: his dominion is an everlasting dominion, which shall not pass away, and his kingdom that which shall not be destroyed."** (Daniel 7:13, 14.) *This one like the son of man* is none other than Jesus himself. (Matthew 24:29-31, 25:31, 32.) *The Ancient of Days* can't be anyone other than *God the Father*, who has always been, and who is all in all. Continuing Daniel's vision; **"But the Saints of the Most High shall take the kingdom, and possess the kingdom forever, even forever and ever. Then I would know the truth of the fourth beast, which was diverse from all the others, exceeding dreadful, whose teeth were of iron, and his nails of brass; which devoured, brake in pieces, and stamped the residue with his feet; and of the ten horns that were in his head, and of the other which came up, and before whom three fell; even of that horn that had eyes, and a mouth that spake very great things, whose look was more stout than his fellows. I beheld and the same horn made war with the Saints, and prevailed against them; until the Ancient of Days came, and judgment was given to the Saints of the Most High; and the time came that the Saints possessed the kingdom. Thus he said, the fourth beast shall be the fourth kingdom upon earth, which shall be diverse from all kingdoms, and shall devour the whole earth, and shall tread it down and brake it in pieces, And the ten horns out of this kingdom are ten kings that shall arise; and another shall arise after them; and he shall be diverse from the first, and he shall subdue three kings. And he shall speak great words against the Most High, and shall wear out the Saints of the Most High, and think to change times and laws; and they shall be given into his hand until a time and times and the dividing of time. But the judgment shall sit, and they shall take away his dominion, to consume and to destroy it unto the end. And the kingdom and dominion, and the greatness of the kingdom under the whole heaven, shall be given to the people of the Saints of the Most High, whose Kingdom is an everlasting Kingdom, and all dominions shall serve and obey him. Hitherto is the end of the matter. As for me Daniel, my** cogitations much troubled me, and my countenance changed in me: But I kept the matter in my heart." (Daniel 7:18-28.)

THESE THINGS TAKE PLACE ON THE EARTH

Daniel in his prophecies describes world conditions that take place on the earth. Many of them took place at a future time, before the coming of Jesus Christ; and some are yet to take place at the second coming of Jesus Christ, and the establishment of the Kingdom of Heaven. We know that Daniel was a true prophet because our modern day history also records the same events predicted by him exactly as he said they would happen, all the way down to and including the Roman Empire which was in power at the time of the ministry of Jesus Christ. It was the Romans, *the fourth kingdom upon the earth, who crucified Jesus.* I don't want you to forget that all these things of which Daniel spoke, except for the meeting of the Son of Man, and the Ancient of Days, (Dan. 7:13-14), take place right here on the **Earth.**

Four of these world ruling kingdoms have already come and gone, the fifth and final world ruling kingdom is not far off. You can rely on the word of God spoken through his prophets. The Babylonian, Medio Persian, Greco Macedonian, and the Roman empires have all had their day. We are still greatly influenced by the Roman era today. Let us look again at one of the prophecies made by Daniel, the one where he reveals the time of the coming of the world ruling Kingdom of God. Notice, "**And in the days of these kings, shall the God of heaven set up a kingdom which shall never be destroyed; and the kingdom shall not be left to other people, but it shall break in pieces and consume all those kingdoms, and it shall stand forever.**"(Dan. 2:44.) This kingdom is none other than the Kingdom of Heaven spoken of by Jesus himself. (Mt. 5:3, 10). Jesus also revealed it to John, read it in Revelation chapters 5 and 11. This will be the fifth and final world ruling empire. It's King will be none other than Jesus, the Son of Man. Notice, "**When the Son of Man shall come in his glory, and all the Holy Angels with him, then shall he sit upon the throne of his glory. And before him shall be gathered all nations; and he shall separate the one from another, as a shepherd divideth his sheep from the goats: And he shall set the sheep on his right hand, but the goats on the left. Then shall the King say to them on his right hand, come, ye blessed of my father; inherit the kingdom prepared for you from the foundation of the world. Then shall he say also unto them on the left hand, Depart from me ye cursed, into everlasting fire, prepared for the devil and his angels**".

(Mt. 25:31-34, 41.) Yes, my friend, the throne upon which the Son of Man shall sit is none other than the throne of David. David's throne is here on the earth. Listen to the words of the angel Gabriel in announcing the birth and destiny of Jesus. **"And in the sixth month the angel Gabriel was sent from God unto a city of Galilee, named Nazareth. To a virgin espoused to a man whose name was Joseph, of the house of David; and the virgin's name was Mary. And the angel came in unto her and said, hail, thou that art highly favoured, the Lord is with thee; 'blessed art thou among women. And when she saw him, she was troubled at his saying, and cast in her mind what manner of salutation this should be. And the angel said unto her, fear not, Mary, for thou hast found favour with God, and, behold thou shalt conceive in thy womb and bring forth a son, and thou shalt call his name Jesus, He shall be great and shall be called the Son of the Highest: and the Lord God shall give unto him the throne of his Father David; and he shall reign over the house of Jacob forever; and of his kingdom there shall be no end."** Lk. 1:26-33.

The angel Gabriel confirmed the prophecy made by Isaiah and Jeremiah. Notice Isaiah's prophecy; **"For unto us a child is born, unto us a son is given; and the government shall be upon his shoulder: and his name shall be called wonderful, counselor, the mighty God, the everlasting father, the prince of peace. Of the increase of his government and peace there shall be no end, upon the throne of David, and upon his kingdom, to order it, and to establish it with judgment and with justice from henceforth, even forever. The zeal of the Lord of hosts will perform this."** (Isa. 9:6, 7.) God's promises never fail; if he promises it he will do it, nothing or nobody can prevent it from coming to pass. Listen to Jeremiah's prophecy concerning the throne of David; **"And the word of the Lord came unto Jeremiah, saying, Thus saith the Lord; if ye can break my covenant of the day, and my covenant of the night, and that there should not be day and night in their season; then may also my covenant be broken with David my servant, that he should not have a son to reign upon his throne; and with the Levites the priests, my ministers."** (Jeremiah 33:19-21.) The Almighty God boasts that if you can break his covenant of day and night so that they do not come in their season, then may his covenant with David also be broken. (Emphasis mine.) So my friend, just as sure as day follows night, and night follows day, that is how sure we can be that *God will send Jesus Christ back to this earth to sit upon the throne of David forever.* Can you believe it?

Jesus Christ demonstrated when he was on earth just how man should and can exercise dominion. Remember the raging Sea? (Mt. 8:24-27.) Remember the ten lepers? (Lk. 17:12-19.) Remember Lazarus? (Jn. 11:38-44.) Remember the blind man? (Jn. 9:6, 7.) Whatever the challenge, Jesus proved that he was more than able to overcome it through the power given him by the Father. And now that he has overcome arch enemy death, defeated man's accuser Satan the devil, and proven that he is worthy of the high and lofty position for which man was made; (Gen. 1:26-28), God the Father has entrusted all power in his hand. (Mt. 28:18.) Not only did he overcome Satan and death, but he gave his life, the just for the unjust, in order to pay the penalty for all mankind, and free them from the curse brought on all the descendants of the first man Adam. (Ro. 8:2.) As stated in the words of the apostle Paul, **"But now is Christ risen from the dead, and become the first fruits of them that slept. For since by man came death, (the penalty for sin brought on by Adam), by man came also the resurrection of the dead, (the result of Jesus' resurrection from the dead.) For as in Adam all die, even so in Christ shall all be made alive."** (1 Cor. 15:20-22.) Yes, my friend, God has not changed his mind; it is still the same as it was at man's inception, that man should have dominion over the earth. He said it, (Gen. 1:26), and when God has said something there is no power in the universe that can prevent it from coming to pass. (Isa. 40:8, 55:11.) So prepare yourself friend, a *King is coming soon, sooner than you think*, he is going to set up a government here that will rule all nations with a rod of iron. (Rev. 19:15, 16.)

MAN CANNOT GOVERN HIMSELF

The entire history of mankind stands as proof that man cannot rule or govern mankind or the universe by himself. Even there in the Garden of Eden, with just Adam and Eve, two human beings, they were unable to govern or control themselves. They allowed Satan to influence them and direct their actions, contrary to the instructions of their creator and maker. Since Eden man has had almost 6,000 years to prove himself capable of governing himself, and exercising the dominion that the Almighty made him for. Instead man has taken on more and more the nature of his adversary Satan. The nature of man can easily be summed up in four words, vanity, jealousy, lust, and greed. These four words describe Satan to a tee. That is why he was thrown out of his high and lofty position as, *"the Cherub that covereth."* (Ez. 28:14.) His vain idea of taking over something that was not his and becoming, *"like the Most High"* has been deeply implanted in the mind of mankind, and many have embraced the idea of, *"going up to heaven."* The first attempt by mankind to accomplish this vain idea was discouraged by the Most High God when he confused the language of those constructing the Tower of Babel. (Gen. 11:7, 8.) God the creator does not need man's expertise in heaven. He created him to have and exercise dominion over the earth, and the Sea, and the things in his (man's) dimension. But man must first learn to exercise dominion over himself. He has to learn that the only way to have dominion over and control the things that the creator has created, is to do it the creator's way.

God knows how to control all things whether they are spiritual or material, for he is the God of all spirits, and the God of all flesh. All things were made by him. He is the *"self existing one"* with absolute power over all things. There are many spirits, just as there are many types of fleshly or carnal beings. Each of these beings has a spirit that makes it what it is. None are self-sustaining; they all have their being in the Most High God. Acts 17:28 says, **"For in him we live and move and have our being."** This portion of scripture applies to every living thing, whether in heaven, on earth, in the sea, or in outer space. Remember, God, (the creator) is maker of *all things in the universe,* whether animate or inanimate, material or spiritual. It is because of the strength of the Lord that all things exist. Even the Moon and the Stars, the Sun and the planets are held in place by the might and power of the creator. Notice; **"To whom then will ye liken me, or shall I be equal? Saith the Holy One. Lift up your eyes on high, and behold who has created these things, that bringeth out their host by number: He calleth them all by name by the greatness of his might, for that he is strong in power; not one faileth."** Isa. 40:25, 26.

Understand the words of the Lord recorded by the prophet, the phrase, *"lift up your eyes on high and behold"* tells us that all we have to do is to look in order to determine the maker; and, *"these things"* could be the heavenly host of Stars, Planets, Sun, and Moon, that the creator stretched out **"as a tent to dwell in."** Isa. 40:22. *Anyone possessing search power as this, and also having the ability to measure the waters in the hollow of his hand, and comprehend the dust of the earth in a measure, and weigh the mountains in scales, is worthy of all our praise and worship. His power is absolute.* All things have their being in him, even Jesus the acknowledged Son of God. A witness to this fact can be found in John 5:26; **"For as the father hath life in himself; so hath he given to the Son to have life in himself."** Where did Jesus get his life from? *The Father.* Verse 30 of John 5 continues, **"I can of mine own self do nothing."** Jesus was willing to glorify the Father by giving him credit for all things he had been granted power to do. Even to the point of giving up his life that the will of the Father be done. (Mt. 26:39-42.)

This brings us to the main reason why mankind cannot govern himself. He wants to govern his way, you know, so he can boast as he does in the song, *"I did it my way."* I am reminded of the year 1945, when the so-called United Nations met, I believe it was in San Francisco, to draw up a plan whereby the world would be assured of **lasting peace.** *A strong hand from somewhere was needed, they agreed, in order to establish a lasting peace.* This they agreed was mankind's only chance of warding off annihilation of all flesh from planet earth. (**Only a few weeks before, the Allies had exploded the Atom bombs over Japan.**) If you were around when all this happened then you know that there has been well over 40 wars since then, and as I write this message we are on the brink of another. **Man's last hope does not depend on his ability to establish peace, but on God's will for him (man) to have peace.** In spite of mankind's weakness God has said through the Psalmist: **"The meek shall inherit the earth and delight themselves in the abundance of peace."** (Psalms 37:11; Matthew 5:5.) Yes, in spite of man's inability to govern himself and establish a lasting peace, peace will suddenly break out all over the earth, and men will beat their swords into plowshares and their spears into pruning hooks. Hear the word of the prophet; **"And it shall come to pass in the last days, that the Mountain of the Lord's house shall be established in the top of the mountains,** (*a mountain in scripture symbolism means a kingdom, see Dan. 2:35, Rev. 13:1, 17:9-11*), **and shall be exalted above the hills; and all nations shall flow unto it. And many people shall go and say, come ye, and let us go up to the mountain of the Lord, to the house of the God of Jacob; and he will teach us of his ways, and we will walk in his paths: For out of Zion shall go forth the law, and the word of the Lord from Jerusalem. And he shall judge among the Nations, and shall rebuke many people: and they shall beat their swords into plow shares, and their spears into pruning hooks; Nation shall not lift up sword against Nation, neither shall they learn war anymore."** (Isa. 2:2-4.)

Just imagine a world wherein there are no more wars, or preparation for war. No more mega-billion dollar budgets to maintain an Army, Navy, and Air Force. No more dooms day weapons to destroy innocent, unsuspecting people. No more screaming air raid sirens, or the deafening roar of giant aircraft overhead, raining down death and destruction upon the earth. Even the animals will be caught up in the abundance of peace. Listen, **"The wolf also shall dwell with the lamb, and the leopard shall lie down with the kid; and the calf and the young lion and the fatling together: and a little child shall lead them. And the cow and the bear shall feed; their young ones shall lie down together: and the lion shall eat straw like the ox. And** the sucking child shall play on the hole of the asp, and the weaned child shall put his hand on the cockatrice den. They shall not hurt nor destroy in all my Holy Mountain: For the earth shall be full of the knowledge of the Lord, as the waters cover the sea." (Isa. 11:6-9.) These things take place right here on the earth. Talk about heaven; it will suddenly be heavenly to dwell on the earth.

Want another witness; notice the prophet Micah's observation of the same end time event; **"But in the last days it shall come to pass, that the mountain of the house of the Lord shall be established in the top of the mountains, and it shall be exalted above the hills, and people shall flow unto it.** (Remember a mountain is sometimes symbolic and means a kingdom). **And many nations shall come and say, come, and let us go up to the mountain of the Lord, and to the house of the God of Jacob; and he will teach us of his ways, and we will walk in his paths; For the law shall go forth of Zion, and the word of the Lord from Jerusalem. And he shall judge among many people, and rebuke strong nations afar off; and they shall beat their swords into plowshares, and their spears into pruning hooks; Nation shall not lift up a sword against nation, neither shall they learn war any more. But they shall sit every man under his vine and under his fig tree; and none shall make them afraid: For the mouth of the Lord of hosts hath spoken it. For all people will walk every one in the name of his God, and we will walk in the name of the Lord our God for ever and ever."** (Micah 4:1-5.) **"In the mouth of two or three witnesses shall every word be established."** (2 Cor. 13:1.) Notice how the words of these two prophets are almost identical. When the Lord wants to put additional emphasis on something he repeats it. Although the prophets Isaiah and Micah shared a period of time during the reign of Jotham, Ahaz, and Hezekiah, the Lord showed them the same vision concerning the coming kingdom of heaven. What a world this will be when the will of God is done on earth just as it is in heaven. Remember how Jesus taught his disciples to pray, **"Thy kingdom come, thy will be done in earth, as it is in heaven."** (Mt. 6:10.)

In such a world the perfect will of the creator will be carried out by all, for he will put his laws into the heart, and, as one thinketh in his heart so is he. (Prov. 23:7.) This is what the creator says; **"This is the covenant that I will make with them after those days, saith the Lord, I will put my laws into their hearts, and in their minds will I write them. And their sins and iniquities will I remember no more."** (Heb. 10:16, 17.) Yes, my friend, the great creator God will govern all his creation, and establish peace in the earth, just as he has established peace in heaven (God's throne) and governs it without contest. He will do it by putting his law in the heart and writing it in the mind. There will no longer be a multitude of differing opinions about who and what God is. There will be no controversy over what his will is, nor where he himself is. Hear him through his word; **"For this is the covenant that I will make with the house of Israel after those days saith the Lord; I will put my laws into their mind, and write them in their hearts; and I will be to them a God, and they shall be to me a people; and they shall not teach every man his neighbor, and every man his brother, saying, know the Lord, for all shall know me, from the least to the greatest. For I will be merciful to their unrighteousness, and their sins, and their iniquities will I remember no more."** (Heb. 8:10-12; Jer. 31:31-34.) No more squabbling and fighting between differing denominations of religion about who is right and who is wrong, for the knowledge of the Lord shall be abundant in all the earth. That old serpent, Satan the devil will no longer be around to persuade men that God does not mean what he says, or that to disobey God is to become as wise as he is. We will be ever in his presence, and his glory will be the very light of out lives. When I think of all the wonderful things that the Lord has in store for his people, I cannot help but to ask, O, Lord, how long? How long before death and suffering will be turned into life and joy? When the law of the Lord is put into the mind of men and permanently written in their hearts, there will be no place in them for Satan's devices. Notice this word from the Lord; **"And I will give them one heart and I will put a new spirit within you; and I will take the stony heart out of their flesh, and will give them an heart of flesh; that they may walk in my statues, and keep mine ordinances, and do them; and they shall be my people, and I will be their God."** (Eze. 11:19, 20.) God will convert and restore his people, and his creation, for his name sake, he will be sanctified and glorified in the things which he has done, (Read Eze. 36:22-38.) Note especially verses 26, 27, 28. God has spoken, his word has gone forth, all things shall be restored, all things to the word and will of the Almighty Creator God. Man has tried his way since he was put out of the Garden of Eden. Man's way has not worked, he has continually brought heartache and disaster upon himself and his surroundings, but he shall be saved. The Almighty will step in and restore all things through the Lord Jesus Christ. (Acts 3:21.) Even so come quickly Lord Jesus!

Wardell N Johnson
296 west 150th Place
Harvey, IL 60426-1470